The Christian
Attitude
Toward War

Loraine Boettner

Presbyterian and Reformed Publishing Company
Phillipsburg, New Jersey

Copyright © 1985
Presbyterian and Reformed Publishing Company

First Printed 1940
Third Edition 1985

Scripture quotations are from the American Standard Version of 1901.

Printed in the United States of America

Library of Congress Cataloging-in-Publication Data

Boettner, Loraine, 1901–
   The Christian attitude toward war.

   1. War—Biblical teaching.   2. War—Religious aspects—Christianity.
3. Pacifism—Religious aspects—Christianity—Controversial literature.
I. Title.
BS680.W2B64   1985   241'.6242   85-17039
ISBN 0-87552-118-5 (pbk.)

Other titles by Loraine Boettner:

The Reformed Doctrine of Predestination
Studies in Theology
Roman Catholicism
The Millennium
Immortality
A Harmony of the Gospels
The Reformed Faith

Contents

1

Introduction

To the people of our day has been given the privilege of living during some of the most momentous crises in the history of the world. Within the lifetime of one generation our nation has been engaged in two world wars and two smaller wars, the Korean and the Vietnam Wars, with their attendant large-scale destruction of life and property. Many people are genuinely puzzled as to the meaning of war and as to what the attitude of the Christian toward it should be. Because of this lack of understanding, and because much of the religious and political freedom that we enjoy was won through wars sanctioned by the church, the discussion of the whole war question is of primary importance.

Sometimes we hear it said that all war is wrong—wrong for the defenders as well as for the aggressors—and that even when waged with the sincere purpose of restraining evil, it tends to produce greater evils than those against which it is directed. Those propositions, we submit, simply are not true. We hold that there is such a thing as a just war—just on the part of those who defend their lives and their homes against unprovoked aggression, but sinful on the part of those who make the attack. To cite only a few instances: If the people of Europe had not resisted the Mohammedan invasions, Europe would have been conquered and, humanly speaking, Christianity would have been stamped out. If at the time of the Reformation the Protestants had not resisted the Roman Catholic persecutions, crimes such as were practiced so freely in the Spanish and Italian Inquisitions would have become common over all of Europe, and Protestantism would have been destroyed. If the American colonists had not fought for their rights, this country would not have gained its independence. In international affairs, as in individual affairs, it often happens that there is an innocent party and a guilty party, although in most cases the guilt is not altogether on one side. And of course there have been many senseless, stupid, inexcusable wars in which neither side was at all concerned about righteousness.

We want to be neither pacifists nor militarists. We would define a pacifist as one who will not sanction or take part in any war, no matter what the occasion or the apparent justification—one who is for peace at any price. And we would define a militarist as one who favors heavy military armaments, primarily for purposes of aggression against other nations. We expect to show that the position that should be taken by anyone who is a true Christian and also a loyal citizen lies somewhere between those two extremes.

It should not be necessary to say that we hate war as do all right-minded people. We hope that our country may never have to engage in another. We desire peace, but we realize there are some things worse than war. We desire peace, but not the kind that is found in the slave camp or the cemetery. It is true that Christ came as the Prince of Peace, and that His followers should strive to promote peace by all lawful means. And for that reason it may seem strange that any professed Christian should enter a protest against the modern pacifist movement. Anyone who does speak against it doubtless will be misunderstood by some. We believe, however, that that movement is dangerous, and that it has no necessary or legitimate part in the evangelical program.

Since the conclusions we reach concerning these problems affect so vitally our attitude toward present-day national and international happenings, and since some people are inclined to take the view that war is always and everywhere wrong, it is important that we have a clear understanding as to what the Christian attitude toward war should be.

2

The Present Crisis[1]

In the year 1848 Karl Marx and Frederich Engles declared war on the entire human race when they published the *Communist Manifesto*. Their opening words were, "A Specter is haunting Europe—the specter of Communism." With these words they laid down the gauntlet and called the world to war. They declared war on mankind. At first they had only brush-fire incidents, clandestine meetings, and failed attempts. But in 1917 Vladimir Lenin delivered Russia into the hands of the Communists. Then at last they had a staging point, a launching pad, a starting place, for world conquest by Communism.

In the *Communist Manifesto* the battle cry was signaled

1. The material in this chapter is taken from a sermon, *The Unholy War*, by Dr. D. James Kennedy, pastor of the Coral Ridge Presbyterian Church, Fort Lauderdale, Florida, delivered February 13, 1983, with a short section from another sermon, *The Soviet Threat*, delivered September 11, 1983. It is quoted by permission.

with these words: "Workers of the world, unite. You have nothing to lose but your chains." Note carefully who it was that was to unite. Workers of Russia? Workers of Eastern Europe? Workers of China? Workers of Cuba? No! "Workers of the *world*, unite"! The Communist movement is a worldwide proletarian revolution, and it will be satisfied with nothing less than the total conquest of the world. War was declared 135 years ago. In the Communist double talk they have continued that same battle cry to the present day. They use terms to mean exactly the opposite of what we mean by them. For example, they talk about peace, but the "peace" of which they speak is simply another act, another form of war. The only "real peace," they declare, will come when the last capitalist nation shall have succumbed to the dictatorship of the proletariat.

Do you remember the words of Lenin in 1924? Right before he died he said, "First, we will take Eastern Europe—Next the masses of Asia. Then we will encircle that last bastion of Capitalism, the United States of America. We shall not have to attack. It will fall like an overripe fruit into our hand." Corrupted from within! overripe fruit! The war has already begun.

Do you remember the words of the famous Soviet strategist, Dimitry Z. Manuilsky? They are most appropriate for this day of huge marches for peace. He said, "There will be electrifying overtures and unheard of concessions. The Capitalistic countries, stupid and decadent, will rejoice to co-operate in their own destruction. They will leap at another chance to be friends. As soon as their guard is down, we shall smash them with our clenched fist!" The only peace they know is the peace that will come when the last bit of opposition to Communism shall have been ground into the dust under the heel of tyranny. Then there shall be "peace"; the peace of the grave, the peace of the well-fed bear lying down to sleep. Until that time, my friend, we are at war.

The Communistic dialectic requires that it be called different things. It may be called "hot war"; it may be called "cold war"; it may be called "detente"; it may be called "cooperation"; but whatever it is called it is simply another form of war. It is the dialectic in operation: two steps forward, one step back; two steps farther forward and one step back. And every time they take a step back the Western world breathes a great sigh of relief and says, "Ah, they have changed. Isn't it wonderful? The Communists are mellowing. We can now get back to our own pleasures. We shall not have to trouble our minds about them anymore." But we read in the Scriptures, "For when they shall say, Peace and safety, then sudden destruction cometh upon them."

Khrushchev, after declaring that the Soviet Union would bury us, said it may not be you, but your grandchildren shall most certainly live under Communism—and that was a generation ago! He was talking about *our children today!*

Communists think in a different way, and Americans are easily deceived by their double talk and their doublethink. We do not understand it. For example, what is "diplomacy"? In the West, we are used to thinking of two possible stages of affairs. We can either be at war, in which case diplomatic relationships are broken, or we can be at peace, wherein diplomatic relationships have been reestablished and we are involved heavily in diplomacy. So the alternatives are clear: we either have war or we have diplomacy. And for every American who thinks that way the Communists would chuckle and laugh at our stupidity. You see, to a Communist, "diplomacy" is simply another phase of war. It is the fifth force. There is the army, navy, air force, marines, and the diplomats that are part of the war-making machine of Communism.

The head of the Russian delegation to the United Nations defected a few years ago and pointed out that more than half of the diplomats at the UN from the Soviet Union were members of the KGB; they were nothing other than professional spies. They were not here for diplomacy. They have simply been waging a different type of war than was ever known before.

We have now made legal the Communist party in America. What are its purposes? Its ostensible and declared purposes are to improve the lot of the working man. This is the promise that has been made over and over again by Communists, and yet the lot of the working man deteriorates wherever they seize power.

The Soviets have had a magnificent ability to deceive. They have kept people from knowing what they are or what they are about until it is too late. I have had people from Estonia, Latvia, Poland, Cuba, and many other countries, say to me, "We didn't know until the iron curtain suddenly fell and we were trapped." People vainly hide themselves, trembling behind closed doors to escape the specter of Communism. As one person said, "A specter walks through the earth—a soulless bloodstained apparition of death."

Communism finds its greatest adversary in Jesus Christ. In the early days of Communism, Lenin formed the Comintern, the Communist International, for the communization of every nation in the world. In that first meeting they drew up the "Ten commandments of Communism." Their first commandment declares what is the chief enemy of Communism. What is its chief enemy—or shall we say, Who is it? Capitalism? The United States? Our economic free enterprise theory? According to the first of the ten commandments of the first Comintern, the chief enemy of Communism is the Christian clergyman!

The Bible says that Satan goes about through the world as a roaring lion, seeking whom he may devour. There are many people who laugh at that and say, "What a foolish thing. Nothing like that is happening." My friends, you should have been in Cambodia in the last several years where four million people were consumed by that lion. You should have been in Vietnam where hundreds of thousands of people were chased out into the open sea by that lion. You should have been in China where sixty million were killed by that lion. You should have been in the Ukraine when virtually the entire Ukrainian population was systematically starved to death by that lion as Stalin forced his will upon those people. It is very, very real.

Remember the words of Lenin. He said Eastern Europe would be absorbed first, then the masses of Asia. The Americas would fall until the United States was surrounded, the last bastion of capitalism. He said America, too, would fall, and that without a fight. "It will fall into our hands like overripe fruit."

What would life under Communism be like? First of all, all people who opposed Communism would be sent to labor camps or would be killed. The first modern city or country the Communists ever took over was Paris,[2] but their control was short-lived. They were overthrown, but Marx and Lenin made it clear that there was only one reason they did not hold onto Paris: *they did not kill enough people.* Thus was born the Communist doctrine that all potential counterrevolutionary elements must be disposed of. You saw it work recently in Cambodia. The city people were systematically killed in a genocide—two million of them.

America has the largest potential counterrevolutionary population of any country in the world for two reasons:

2. Shortly after the close of the First World War.

(1) it has the largest middle class in the world; (2) it has the largest Christian population in the world. Both of these would be targeted for extinction. It is estimated by experts that some 60 million Americans would be killed, all potential leaders in a revolution. I have no illusions about what would happen to me. I do not have very many illusions about surviving until that time. But I want you to understand that the same would probably happen to almost all of you.

Freedom would be gone. For those who remain, there would be the issuance of something totally foreign to an American—an internal passport without which and the permission of the Communist party no one could go from one town to another. Should you be found anywhere without that passport, you could be cast into prison.

All churches would be closed. You ask, "Does not the Soviet Union allow freedom of religion?" Not really. Not at all. They are at total war with religion. They have closed down about 90 percent of all the churches, about 90 percent of the seminaries and monasteries. They leave a few open as a pretense.

Under Khrushchev three rules were passed: (1) every member of the Communist party must be an atheist; (2) no child under eighteen could enter a church; (3) any parent caught teaching his child anything about religion before the age of eighteen would have the child taken away for life. But in spite of these, they have not been able to stamp out religion.

That is a brief description of what would happen in America. There would be no semblance of religious freedom because that is only for propaganda purposes for the West right now. But if they took over the world, there would be no one left to impress. Propaganda would give way to persecution and execution. There would be no further need for pretense. All freedom would be gone not only here but also in the Soviet Union.

If we are going to overcome that threat we must realize that we are at war *now*. It will inevitably be a war to the end. There is no containment; there is no living in cooperation; Communists are set on nothing other than world conquest. Ultimately, Communism can be destroyed only by the power of the gospel and by an understanding of what they are and what they intend to do. Only in this way will Communism ever be turned back.

We have a religion. We are called to be soldiers. We have a goal of world conquest—not with Molotov cocktails, tanks, or bombs; not by murder and enslavement—but by the gospel of peace, by the Good News of eternal salvation. Not by enslaving people, but by setting them free. One or the other of these views is going to dominate in this world. It is going to depend on which group is more committed to its task.

Finally, I think it is vitally important that every American know that the cause of secular humanism in America is nothing other than a disguised version of world Communism. The two represent exactly the same thing. Secular, atheistic humanism—which is becoming ever more dominant and regnant in America—is nothing but Communism waiting to be crowned with its political rights. It is atheistic. It holds the same evolutionary view of man as an animal. It has no absolute moral views. It is socialistic. It views a future world government that is inevitably Communistic. It is, indeed, fostering the Communistic view on America from within. It is corrupting the people of this country, especially our youth. It is corrupting our courts, our schools, our government, and our media. It is bringing about the corruption that will cause America to fall like overripe fruit into their hands.

Unless Christians get serious about the task to which Christ has called us, unless we demonstrate that our commitment is as great as or greater than theirs, there is no doubt we shall fail. The early Christian church overthrew the enormous monolith of the pagan Roman Empire because they had a commitment to Christ that was life consuming. They felt that Christ was all in all. Their great purpose for life was to make Him known to other people, to love Him and to share Him with a lost and needy world.

What will it be, my friend: Will our children most certainly live under Communism? It depends upon *you and me.* We must realize that war has been declared—an unholy war—and the war has already begun.

3

What the Old Testament Teaches Concerning War

In all matters of controversy among Christians the Scriptures are accepted as the highest court of appeal. Historically they have been the common authority of Christendom. We believe that they "are given by inspiration of God, to be the rule of faith and practice" (The Westminster Confession of Faith I, 2); that they contain one harmonious, consistent, and sufficiently complete system of doctrine; and that it is our duty to trace out this consistency by a careful investigation of the meaning of particular passages. No person, acting merely on his own observations and judgments, can know what are the basic principles of the plan that God is following. All philosophical speculation and emotional sentiment should be held in abeyance until we have first heard the testimony of Scripture. And when we have heard that testimony we should submit. Would that we had more people with that noble characteristic of the Bereans, who, when Paul preached to them, searched the Scriptures daily to see whether or not the things that he spoke were so.

The question at issue is simply this: What do the Scriptures teach concerning war? We say that this is the issue, even though liberals in the church, who in the main are the sponsors of the modern pacifist movement, do not feel themselves bound to take seriously the teachings of either the Old or the New Testament. In this chapter we shall consider the teaching of the Old Testament, and in the next chapter, the New.

Time and again in the Old Testament we read that God gave the Israelites the direct command to go into battle against their enemies and that He gave them the victory. "Jehovah is a man of war: Jehovah is his name. Pharaoh's chariots and his host hath he cast into the sea," sang Moses after the Israelites had been delivered from the Egyptians (Exod. 15:3, 4).

Almost immediately after the Israelites came out of Egypt they were attacked by the Amalekites. Israel was at that time a theocracy, the purest form of government, with God speaking through His prophet and ruling directly in the affairs of the nation. Thus guided, Moses chose the young man Joshua to lead the army. During the battle, as the hands of Moses were held up to God in prayer, the Israelites prevailed, and when his hands were let down, the Amalekites prevailed. With the assistance of Aaron and Hur his hands were held up until evening, and the victory was won (Exod. 17:8-16).

After the Israelites had spent forty years in the wilderness they received the direct command from God to go into the land of Palestine and drive out or destroy the inhabitants. They were told that they did not go in their own strength, but that Jehovah would go before them, and that the battle was not theirs but Jehovah's. They were also told not to make any alliances with the inhabitants of the land and that if they disobeyed that command, those degraded people would be a snare and a trap to them, a scourge in their side and thorns in their eyes, until they themselves would be corrupted and would perish (Num. 33:50-56; Josh. 1:1-9).

As Joshua stood before the walls of Jericho he met a stranger with a drawn sword in his hand, whom he soon discovered to be Jehovah, the Angel of the Covenant, the same one who had visited Abraham at the Oaks of Mamre, who had wrestled with Jacob at Peniel, and who had appeared to Moses in the burning bush. Thus Joshua received directly from God specific instructions for the conquest and destruction of the city (Josh. 5:13–6:27). And it is further true that if we pursue the theophany into the New Testament, we find that this was none other than the Lord Jesus Christ, the second person of the Trinity, the active agent of the Godhead in all creation. This is the one who stood before Joshua and gave him detailed instructions for the taking of Jericho and for the complete destruction of that people—men, women, and children—with the exception of Rahab and her family.

If anyone today is inclined to feel that the wars against the Philistines were unjust, let him consider the declarations of Scripture and the evidence from archaeology concerning the abominable sins of those people, the sex crimes practiced even in connection with their religion, the burning of their infant sons and daughters as human sacrifices to Baal and Molech, and their fiendish cruelty in war; in contrast with which their forthright execution by the Israelites seems manly and dignified, if not even merciful. There we find, as in the cases of Sodom and Gomorrah, not merely individuals but whole tribes too degraded and sinful to live. And the Israelites were but the divinely appointed means for their extermination.

Deborah, the prophetess, and Barak, the captain of the army, were directed of God in the battle against Sisera and the Canaanites (Judg. 4:1-23); and in Deborah's song of victory we hear judgment pronounced against the city of Meroz, whose inhabitants had refused to help in the battle:

Curse ye Meroz, said the angel of Jehovah,
Curse ye bitterly the inhabitants thereof.
Because they came not to the help of Jehovah,
To the help of Jehovah against the mighty (Judg. 5:23).

Gideon received a vision in which he was directed to free the people from the Midianites, and the battle was so ordered that the Israelites knew most definitely that they had not won by their own strength, but that Jehovah had given them the victory (Judg. chaps. 6–7). God commanded the destruction of the Amalekites, and when King Saul carried out his mission only halfheartedly, sparing Agag the king, we read that "Samuel hewed Agag in pieces before Jehovah in Gilgal" (I Sam. 15:1-33). David was providentially called to go and fight the giant Goliath, who was defying the God of the armies of Israel. Jehovah delivered Goliath into his hands, and Israel was freed from Philistine domination (I Sam. 17:1-54). Soon after David became king, the Philistines came up to pillage the land. In II Samuel 5:19, 20 we read, "And David inquired of Jehovah, saying, Shall I go up against the Philistines? Wilt thou deliver them into my hand? And Jehovah said unto David, Go up; for I will certainly deliver the Philistines into thy hand. And David came to Baal-perazin, and David smote them there; and he said, Jehovah hath broken mine enemies before me."

Many of the Psalms are prayers to God for guidance in war or hymns of thanksgiving to God for victories in war. "Let God arise, let his enemies be scattered; Let them also that hate him flee before him. As smoke is driven away, so drive them away: As wax melteth before the fire, so let the wicked perish at the presence of God. . . . Kings of armies flee, they flee; And she that tarrieth at home divideth the spoil. . . . The chariots of God are twenty thousand, even thousands upon thousands: The Lord is among them, as in Sinai, in the sanctuary" (Ps. 68:1-2, 12, 17). David acknowledged that his skill in battle was a gift from God: "Blessed be Jehovah my rock, who teacheth my hands to war, And my fingers to fight" (Ps. 144:1).

There is absolutely no question that in the Old Testament wars were sanctioned as a means of gaining righteous ends. At other times they were used as severe disciplinary measures against the Israelites when they went into apostasy, and God allowed them to be conquered by the Midianites, the Philistines, or the Assyrians (Judg. 6:1; 13:1; Isa. 10: 5-14). In such events God is revealed as Creator, Lawgiver, Father, and Judge, and also as the Lord God of battle. He commands Israel to go to war, and goes before her, but (and this is the important point) *Israel must not go before God.* When Israel was so presumptuous as to go to war after God had forbidden it, she was disastrously defeated (cf. Num. 14:39-45; Josh. 7:1–8:29; I Sam. 28:15-19).

Sometimes we hear the sixth commandment quoted to prove that all war is wrong. But the same God who in the twentieth chapter of Exodus said, "Thou shalt not kill," which literally means, "Thou shalt not commit murder," says in the twenty-first chapter, "He that smiteth a man so that he dieth, shall surely be put to death." And centuries before that, the commandment had been given, "Whoso sheddeth man's blood, by man shall his blood be shed" (Gen. 9:6). The command against wilful murder is to be made effective by the sentence of capital punishment against the offender. The judge who sentences the criminal to death is no more guilty of murder than he would be guilty of robbery were he to sentence him to pay a fine. Otherwise there would be no possible way to maintain public justice. And the policeman or the soldier who defends his country, like the judge who protects society, does not act with a malicious motive to avenge a personal wrong, but with an altruistic motive for public safety. He performs his duty not as an individual but as an officer of the state. And in the Scriptures war among nations is given the same status as capital punishment among individuals.

There is nothing in the Old Testament that even suggests that it is inconsistent to be at one and the same time a soldier and a follower of the Lord God of hosts. There are some thirty-five or more references throughout the Old Testament where God has commanded the use of armed force in carrying out His divine purposes. The Scriptures reveal God as a God of war as well as a God of peace. And to say, as some pacifists do, that war defies the righteousness of God is not only presumptuous but equivalent to saying that God Himself is unrighteous. For the Bible, the very Book that we as Christians profess to accept as "the only infallible rule of faith and practice," declares that on certain occasions God not only has permitted war but has commanded it.

There is, however, in the Scriptures no glorification of war or of the warrior as such. On several occasions the Israelites were refused permission to take booty or to glory in their achievements. David, the foremost warrior in the Old Testament, was forbidden to build the temple of Jehovah because he had shed so much blood. War was looked upon as a grim and terrible necessity in the hands of God for the restraint and punishment of national sins. It was to be avoided if possible, and it was never to be glorified. And that is the attitude that we should take toward it today.

4

What the New Testament Teaches Concerning War

The New Testament gives no direct teaching on the subject of war, although it does make it plain that the civil government—whether kingdom, empire, or republic, it does not say—is divinely established so that as citizens we are to recognize its authority and to perform our duties toward it. That there should be a difference of emphasis and objective between the Old and the New Testament is quite natural, since there was a difference of dispensations, and since the former was written to and about a nation, while the latter was written to individuals and to a nonpolitical body known as the church. The ceremonial laws of the Old Testament had been fulfilled and had passed away, but the moral laws remained in full force. The two Testaments fit together in perfect harmony. Even the teaching of Jesus concerning love to our fellow men does not rise higher than the passage quoted by Him from Leviticus 19:18: "Thou shalt love thy neighbor as thyself." When rightly under-

18

stood the two Testaments are supplementary, not contradictory. The silence of the New Testament on the subject of war apparently rests on the assumption that the subject had been adequately treated and did not call for any addition or modification.

It has been alleged by pacifists that the teachings of Jesus forbid the Christian to take part in war. We are convinced, however, that the allegation finds no support either in Christ's words or in His conduct. In the first place it fails to take into consideration His teaching concerning the authority of Scripture. That He considered the Old Testament fully inspired is abundantly clear. He quoted it as such and based His teachings upon it. One of His clearest statements is found in John 10:35, where, in controversy with the Jews, His defense takes the form of an appeal to Scripture; and after quoting a statement He adds the significant words, "And the Scriptures cannot be broken." His Bible, the only Bible that existed in His day, was the Old Testament. The reason it was worthwhile for Him, or that it is worthwhile for us, to appeal to Scripture is that it "cannot be broken"— and the word here translated "broken" is the common one for breaking the law, or the Sabbath, meaning to annul, or deny, or withstand its authority. For Him an appeal to Scripture was an appeal to an authority whose determination was final, even to its minute details. Whenever Christ or the apostles quoted Scripture, they thought of it as the living voice of God and therefore divinely authoritative. In His stinging rebuke to the Sadducees, "Ye do err, not knowing the Scriptures" (Matt. 22:29), the very thing that He pointed out was that their error came, not because they followed the Scriptures, but precisely because they did not follow them. So common was their use, and so unquestionable was their authority, that in the fiercest conflict Jesus needed no other weapon than the final "It is written!"

(Matt. 4:4, 7, 10; Luke 4:4, 8; 24:26). Hence if we take Christ as an authority, we will also take the entire Old Testament as an authority. He hands it to us and tells us that it is the Word of God and that the prophets spoke by the Holy Spirit. By His numerous quotations He has welded it to the New Testament so that they now form one unified Bible. The two Testaments have but one voice. They must stand or fall together.

But let us consider more specifically the teachings of Jesus. We often hear Matthew 5:39 quoted to prove the pacifist position: "Whosoever smiteth thee on thy right cheek, turn to him the other also." This verse teaches that within reasonable limits it is often better to suffer a personal injustice than to demand our rights and perhaps precipitate a quarrel or a fight. If we are truly Christian, we will live unselfish lives, not always seeking to vindicate our own petty dignity, but returning good for evil. And if the offending person is possessed of even a minimum of manly qualities, such a response makes him ashamed of his conduct so that he is not likely to repeat it. Probably three out of four personal quarrels arise because of misunderstood motives. A reasonable amount of patience on our part, together with the manifestation of a good motive, will go a long way toward smoothing over difficulties.

Furthermore, the injunction to turn the other cheek refers to our individual attitude. A person has the right to sacrifice himself provided he does not exceed reasonable limits; but he does not have the right to sacrifice others. As one writer has said, "I am not to turn my wife's cheek, or the other cheek of the weak and defenseless whom I am called upon to protect. With this in mind, it may be that going into the firing line is in very truth turning the other cheek—letting the enemy smite our cheek rather than that of those we love. Christ turned His other cheek for us. And when it is all over we are to love and forgive the enemy" (Dr. George W. Arms).

Clearly Jesus never intended this saying to be taken literally. When during the trial before the Sanhedrin He was struck, He did not invite further abuse by turning the other cheek, but immediately rebuked the offender with the words, "If I have spoken evil, bear witness of the evil: but if well, why smitest thou me?" (John 18:22, 23). Jesus turned the other cheek in the true sense a short time before the events of His trial when in the garden He returned good for evil by healing the servant whose ear had been cut off by Peter's sword.

Sometimes we hear the Golden Rule quoted to prove that we should not use military force against any people, that we are to do unto others as we would have them do unto us. But in the event of war we have to decide who the "others" are in whose place we are to put ourselves—the lustful, murderous invaders who do not want us to resist them, or our own wives and children who need our protection.

On two occasions Jesus went into the temple and with a show of force poured out the changers' money, overturned their tables, and drove out those who through fraudulent dealings were making the temple a den of robbers. On numerous occasions he met His enemies, the scribes and Pharisees, face to face and denounced them as hypocrites and liars, declaring that they were of their father the devil and were doomed to perdition (Matt. 15:7; 23:33; John 8:44, 45). In the parable of the wicked husbandman He accepted as true and justified the course of action ascribed to the lord of the vineyard (by whom He meant God): "But these mine enemies, that would not that I should reign over them, bring hither, and slay them before me" (Luke 19:27). No one else in Scripture gave more frequent or sterner warnings of the punishment that God will inflict on the wicked. In the well-known judgment scene of Matthew 25, Jesus Himself sits as Judge and passes sentence on His enemies: "Depart from me, ye cursed, into the eternal fire which is prepared for the Devil and his angels" (v. 41). Those are not the words of a pacifist, nor could His enemies have looked upon Him as such.

We are sometimes reminded that we should love our enemies, and we are told that if we do love them we will not go to war against them. But while the Christian is commanded to love his enemies, that does not mean that he cannot defend himself or his loved ones against them. Nor does it necessarily follow that self-defense and love of those who would oppress us are contradictory. The judge who passes sentence on the evildoer may at the same time have a deep sense of pity and sympathy for him. We are indeed to love our enemies; but we cannot love them in the same way, nor with the same intensity, that we love our friends. We can love them in that while we are convinced that they are in the wrong and want to injure us, we nevertheless bear them no hate, and we would honestly like to turn them from their evil course and persuade them to a better way of life.

The pacifist is inclined to be governed more by sentiment and emotion than by the hard facts of life and to overemphasize the love of God at the expense of His justice. While to the righteous God is a God of love, to the wicked He is "a consuming fire" (Deut. 4:24; Heb. 12:29) and will certainly punish sin. The apostle who wrote the great discourse on the love of God as found in I Corinthians 13 also wrote in that same book, "If any man loveth not the Lord, let him be anathema" (16:22). And it is often forgotten that even John 3:16 speaks not only of the love of God but also of His punitive justice, not only of heaven but also of hell. To overemphasize the love of God while neglecting His justice is very dangerous, for instead of arousing the sinner to a true sense of his danger, it only makes him more complacent in his sin.

The believing centurion received no rebuke from Jesus for any sinfulness attaching to his profession as such, and Peter welcomed into the church another centurion, Cornelius, who was "a righteous man and one that feared God" (Acts 10:22). When the soldiers who were converted through the stern preaching of John the Baptist asked what they should do to apply those principles of righteousness in their lives, John uttered not one word of rebuke against their profession; but assuming that they would remain soldiers, as is clearly implied in his injunction that they were to be content with their wages, he warned them against those temptations which are peculiar to soldiers: "Extort from no man by violence, neither accuse any wrongfully, and be content with your wages" (Luke 3:14). In other words, they were engaged in a lawful profession, a necessary profession if law and order were to be maintained throughout the country. They were simply told to do their duty and not to abuse their authority, which certainly was good practical advice. From New Testament times until the present it has been the policy of the church to admit and retain soldiers as Christians in good and regular standing.

In the last discourse that Jesus had with His disciples, we find some significant words in regard to the use of weapons. He reminded them that on their former missionary journey, which was of short extent and among their own people, He had sent them forth without purse, or wallet, or shoes, and that they lacked nothing. But then, in regard to later missionary journeys that they were to make over long distances and among hostile people, he said, "But now, he that hath a purse, let him take it, and likewise a wallet: *and he that hath none, let him sell his cloak and buy a sword*" (Luke 22:36). So important would it be that they have some means of self-defense that, if necessary, they were to sell their coats to secure it. As strange as sword bearing may seem to us who live in a peaceful, settled country such as the United States, where a well-organized police force keeps crime comparatively to a minimum, it was entirely appropriate in that lawless, barbarous age. We get a glimpse of those conditions when Paul tells us that often he was "in perils of robbers, in perils from my countrymen, in perils from the Gentiles, in perils in the city, in perils in the wilderness, in perils in the sea, in perils among false brethren" (II Cor. 11:26). If we lived under such conditions we would have occasion to become much better acquainted with weapons than we now are.

Peter's misuse of his sword a little later, when he struck at a servant of the high priest with the evident intent of killing him but succeeded only in cutting off an ear, does not invalidate this teaching. Jesus' rebuke to Peter was not a command to destroy the sword or to throw it away, but simply, "Put up the sword into the sheath" (John 18:11). The Lord thereby implied that although that was not the proper time or place to use it, since He proposed to surrender Himself voluntarily, there would nevertheless be appropriate occasions for its future use. And the further admonition, "All they that take the sword shall perish with the sword," expresses a truth that has been proved over and over again in everyday life—those who rely on the sword above everything else, those who put their *trust* in the sword, inevitably perish. The gangster who puts his trust in the pistol perishes by the pistol, for the very simple reason that the officers of the law are authorized to take the pistol against him. We are to put our trust in the Lord, although He expects us to use the ordinary means at our disposal for protection against vicious men as definitely as He expects us to use the ordinary means to provide food to keep us from starvation, or to provide clothing and shelter to keep us from the cold.

For too long the picture of Jesus as a weak, inoffensive, harmless person has been allowed to go unchallenged. The New Testament certainly does not present Him as such a person. These characteristics have been inferred (1) partly, no doubt, from His gentle and sympathetic way of dealing with the erring and with those who were afflicted or sorrowful, (2) partly because of His admonition to "resist not him that is evil" (Matt. 5:38, 39, where the context makes it clear that He forbids the taking of revenge, not that He advocates nonresistance in general), and (3) partly because during His public ministry women were drawn with peculiar loyalty to His service and often have been more active than men in the church since that time. It is well to keep in mind that in the ordinary relationships between men and women it is the masculine qualities of strength, initiative, and leadership, and not the feminine qualities, that women admire in men. The disciples and all others who saw and heard Jesus were strongly impressed with His courage, His fearlessness, His tireless energy, and His air of supreme self-confidence and leadership. Repeatedly the Gospel writers use the words "power" and "authority" in regard to Him. From the beginning of His public ministry until He was nailed to the cross He was in courageous opposition to the scribes and Pharisees, showing how they perverted the Scriptures, denouncing them as liars and hypocrites, and exposing their fraudulent practices. Single-handed and alone, He stood against those organized groups that were holding His people in mental and spiritual bondage. In that terrible conflict He was as truly a fighter as was Moses, or David, or Washington, or Grant, or MacArthur, or Eisenhower. He called His disciples not to a life of ease and comfort and safety, but to one of hardship and sacrifice and danger. He sent them out on missions that would take them to the ends of the earth and warned them that they would suffer persecution and in some instances death. Certainly no weakling could have inspired men for such service as that. And for the past two thousand years He has been the dominating influence in our Western world. That He used mental and moral rather than physical force does not alter the fact that He fought, nor does it mean that on appropriate occasions He would not have used physical force. Physical force cannot be regarded as something that is wrong in itself. It is not the kind of force used, but rather the spirit in which it is used, that determines whether or not the encounter is a fight. And the record leaves no doubt but that the purpose of Jesus was to defeat and silence His enemies.

Jesus of course could not sanction war during His earthly ministry without having the whole nature of His kingdom misunderstood. The Jews were in a state of apostasy and were anxiously awaiting a temporal, military messiah who they hoped would place himself at the head of their army, free them from the despised Romans, and restore the kingdom as it had been under David and Solomon. Jesus avoided every appearance of temporal or military power; but even then, at the time of His death, His closest disciples still were not able to grasp the spiritual nature of the kingdom. In the presence of such people any reference to military power would have been entirely misunderstood.

In Romans 13:1-7, Paul gave an emphatic declaration concerning the divinely established authority of the state, which incidentally includes a clear and positive statement against pacifism. He wrote,

> Let every soul be in subjection to the higher powers [that is, to the civil government, whether kingdom, empire, republic, or democracy], for the powers that are are *ordained of God*. Therefore he that withstandeth the power, withstandeth the

ordinance of God; and they that withstand shall receive to themselves judgment. For rulers are not a terror to the good work, but to the evil. . . . For he [the ruler] is *a minister of God* to thee for good. But if thou do that which is evil, be afraid; *for he beareth not the sword in vain* [the sword was used for killing, hence this is the counterpart of the Old Testament command that "whoso sheddeth man's blood, by man shall his blood be shed"]; for he is a minister of God, *an avenger for wrath to him that doeth evil.*

Here we are taught that it is the duty of the state to maintain law and order, if need be, by the sword.

The Roman government of Paul's day, which of course was the government that he had in mind as he wrote, promoted peace throughout the world by force of arms. The emperor was Nero, the persecutor of the Christians, the one under whom Paul eventually was put to death. Paul did not advocate loyalty to the Roman government because of its religious stance (for it was thoroughly pagan, whereas he was Jewish and Christian), but because, all things considered, it was a reasonably good government, maintaining a fair degree of law and order in secular affairs. Although the ruler was a weak and sinful man, he was, nevertheless, in his official capacity, and without knowing it, the *minister of God* in maintaining justice, law, and order. On several occasions Paul himself had appealed to the Roman authority for military protection and had received it; hence he knew whereof he spoke. Despite its faults, the state of law and order that the Roman government maintained was far better than anarchy.

The distinction between the church and the state has been clearly set forth by Dr. Albertus Pieters, former Professor of Theology at Western Theological Seminary, Holland, Michigan.

There are two independent sovereignties, both ordained of

God: the Church and the State. The State is as truly a divine institution as the Church. The State is the trustee of the law, the Church of the Gospel: the former bears the sword for the forcible restraint of sin, the latter holds the secret of the only remedy for sin. The former compels men to abstain from the grosser forms of open sin; the latter inspires them with a hatred of secret sin and a love for holiness. Both are necessary, and neither has the right to interfere with the other.

Jesus had said, "Render unto Caesar the things that are Caesar's, and unto God the things that are God's," and Paul added, "Render unto all their dues: tribute to whom tribute is due; custom to whom custom; fear to whom fear; honor to whom honor" (Rom. 13:7). We are to obey God first and foremost, because He has commanded it; and then, because He has also commanded it, we are to obey the earthly government. We are to remember that Caesar at his best is imperfect and human, and at his worst, thoroughly bad and devilish. The Caesar to whom Jesus commanded the Jews to be obedient was a pagan, unjust, and corrupt. But despite those personal faults, he was the lawful head of the state. The Jews were subject to the Roman Empire and partook of many of the benefits of orderly government. Jesus, therefore, regarded it as their duty to pay the tax and thus help meet the expenses of government. It was perfectly evident that not all of the tax money would be spent for good purposes, but that did not excuse them from paying a reasonable amount.

It often happens that a Caesar, human and fallible as he is, does not know, or deliberately exceeds, his divinely appointed limitations. In such cases if a moral principle is involved, the Christian, like the disciples when brought before their rulers and elders, must choose to obey God rather than men, regardless of the consequences. History is eloquent in declaring that thousands have died martyr's deaths rather than renounce their faith.

In the present age national governments are a moral necessity without which our social institutions could not be preserved and developed. The church does not have the power to collect taxes or to maintain armed forces. Her powers are spiritual and declarative. But the state, possessing the power to collect taxes, has both the right and the duty to maintain police and military protection for the orderly working of society and for the maintenance of peaceful life and worship by the church.

It is the teaching of both the Old Testament and the New that the ruler is "a minister of God," holding office not merely by appointment of man but by the appointment of God (and therefore responsible for doing justice and punishing evil, although often negligent in his duty). "By me kings reign, and princes decree justice. By me princes rule, and nobles, even all the judges of the earth" (Prov. 8:15, 16). "I will establish the throne of his kingdom for ever" (II Sam. 7:13). God, speaking through His prophet Jeremiah, said, "I have given all these lands into the hand of Nebuchadnezzar the king of Babylon, my servant . . . therefore, serve him and his people, and live" (Jer. 27:6, 12). And parallel with this are the words of David who, although already anointed to be the future king of Israel and unjustly persecuted by the wicked Saul, when urged to kill Saul, replied, "Jehovah forbid that I should do this thing unto my lord, Jehovah's anointed"; and again, "For who can put forth his hand against Jehovah's anointed, and be guiltless?" (I Sam. 24:6; 26:9).

We believe not only that God created this world, but that He continues to govern it. Occasionally we see famines, floods, plagues, earthquakes, etc., in which thousands of lives and much property is lost. All of these things occur under His providential control. The perversion of the human mind is such that wealth, luxury, security, prolonged good health, etc., often result in profound spiritual indifference; and God in His wisdom may work out greater good through some of these forms of suffering than without them. And if He permits and uses these things, there is no valid reason why He should not also permit and use war as an instrument of moral government. The suffering caused by war is not necessarily any more severe or prolonged than are those which befall people in other ways.

This in general has been the view held by the various Christian churches concerning the lawfulness of war and the authority of the state in so far as they have attempted to base their position on Scripture. The historic position of Presbyterianism, for instance, has been set forth in these words:

> God, the Supreme Lord and King of all the world, hath ordained civil authorities to be under Him over the people, for His own glory and the public good: and, to this end hath armed them with the power of the sword, for the defense and encouragement of them that are good, and for the punishment of evil doers.

> It is lawful for Christians to accept and execute the office of magistrate, when called thereunto: in the managing thereof, as they ought especially to maintain piety, justice and peace, according to the wholesome laws of each commonwealth; *so, for that end, they may lawfully, now under the New Testament, wage war upon just and necessary occasions* (Westminster Confession of Faith, XXIII, 2, italics ours).

In these words the state is acknowledged to be of divine origin, and its officers are declared to possess "the power of the sword." This is not a sanction for the church to enter war, nor is it directly a sanction by the church for its individual members to enter war, although that permission is implied. It is specifically a sanction for the magistrate—

which would mean primarily the President of the United States, since he is commander-in-chief of the armed forces —to defend this nation in time of crisis. It does not require war, but merely permits it "upon just and necessary occasions." Even on occasions that the magistrate deems just, this merely says that he "may" wage war, which implies the caution that war is not the only alternative in international disputes and that other things should come first, such as diplomatic exchange of opinions, and reasonable compromise. It also suggests that if our nation is being plunged into war for merely selfish or ambitious reasons, we have the right to resist that movement.

In the light of the general and pervasive Scripture teaching, it is quite evident that the objections raised against the Christian's participation in military service are based on emotional or philosophical rather than scriptural grounds. Pacifists are able to argue with some plausibility only when dealing with a few selected passages while keeping out of view the general mass of scriptural evidence bearing on the whole subject. As Christians we take our stand on the interpretation of Scripture as a whole; and so long as we hold to the principle that the Scriptures are to be accepted as the sole authority in matters of faith and practice, there is no valid reason for denying that the magistrate "may lawfully, now under the New Testament, wage war on just and necessary occasions."

5

War Symbolism in the Scriptures and in Hymns

In trying to arrive at a true understanding as to what the Christian attitude toward war is, we should notice that in addition to the direct Scripture teaching, the symbolism used in Scripture is taken largely from the army and the battlefield. The most familiar figure applied to the church is that of an army following Jesus Christ as the great Commander-in-chief. The Book of Revelation, in portraying the future conquest of the world, pictures Christ as a Warrior upon a white horse, followed by the armies of heaven upon white horses: "In righteousness he doth judge and make war. . . . And out of His mouth proceedeth a sharp sword, that with it he should smite the nations: and he shall rule them with a rod of iron" (Rev. 19:11, 15).

Paul admonishes us to put on "the whole armor of God," which includes "the breastplate of righteousness," "the shield of faith, wherewith we may be able to quench all the fiery darts of the evil one," "the helmet of salvation," and "the sword of the Spirit" (Eph. 6:14-17). To Timothy he wrote, "Suffer hardship with me, as a good soldier of Jesus Christ" (II Tim. 2:3). He urges the Christian to "fight the good fight of faith" (I Tim. 6:12) and declares that "we are more than conquerors through him that loved us" (Rom. 8:37).

The pacifists would need to perform a major operation on both the Old and the New Testaments in order to delete passages such as those just cited. They would make it impossible for Paul to bring his career to an end by saying, "I have fought a good fight." Instead they might translate it, "I have played a good hand," or "I have put through a good deal."

Our easygoing and luxury-loving age desires a Christianity that can be set forth under the aspects of beauty, loveliness, meekness, and humility. It is inclined to forget that Christianity, in order to be truly biblical, must have its aspects of sternness and wrath against every wrong. The battle rages between the forces of righteousness, light, and truth on the one side, and those of sin, darkness, and error on the other. In this battle the church of Christ, militant and triumphant, marches as to war.

It is hardly conceivable that the Scriptures should present the Christian life under a symbolism having to do so distinctly with soldiering and warfare and at the same time repudiate the reality for which that symbolism stands as always and everywhere wrong. We cannot imagine the different aspects of the Christian life being set forth through symbolism borrowed from the liquor traffic or the vice rackets.

Equally interesting is the symbolism used in the songs through which the church has worshiped down through the ages. What heart does not thrill to the challenge of "Onward, Christian Soldiers," or "The Son of God Goes

Forth to War, A Kingly Crown to Gain." Listen to the stirring words of the hymn, "Stand Up for Jesus":

> Stand up, stand up for Jesus,
> Ye soldiers of the cross;
> Lift high His royal banner,
> It must not suffer loss:
> From victory unto victory
> His army He shall lead,
> Till every foe is vanquished,
> And Christ is Lord indeed.
>
> Stand up, stand up for Jesus,
> The trumpet call obey;
> Forth to the mighty conflict,
> In this His glorious day:
> Ye that are men now serve Him
> Against unnumbered foes;
> Let courage rise with danger,
> And strength to strength oppose.
>
> Stand up, stand up for Jesus,
> Stand in His strength alone;
> The arm of flesh will fail you,
> Ye dare not trust your own;
> Put on the Gospel armour,
> Each piece put on with prayer;
> Where duty calls, or danger,
> Be never wanting there.
>
> Stand up, stand up for Jesus,
> The strife will not be long;
> This day the noise of battle,
> The next the victor's song:
> To him that overcometh,
> A crown of life shall be;
> He with the King of Glory
> Shall reign eternally.

As one writer has said,

Our pacifist friends are often grieved today because Christianity bristles with so many military terms, because the Church is so often likened to an army, and the Christian to a soldier. They tell us that such a hymn as "Onward Christian Soldiers" should be deleted from our hymnals. But I am glad it is there. I am glad that once in a while in our peaceful worship there comes a strain of martial music and the sound of marching feet. For all of this serves to keep before us a fact that we should never forget, namely, that *Christianity is a war,* a war against sin and selfishness within and against every monstrous evil, against every demon of greed and cruelty and hate which slays the souls of men and makes the world a hell (Dr. C. Waldo Cherry).

6

Historical Aspects

A brief glance at history should convince us that most of the religious and political liberty we enjoy was made possible only through the willingness of our forefathers to struggle for their natural human rights. Our American republic owes its very existence to the brave men who were ready to do battle for home and loved ones and for civil and religious freedom.

If we go back in the history of England and search for her true heroes, we shall find them in that noble body of English Calvinists whose insistence on a purer form of worship and a purer life won for them the nickname "Puritan," to whom the historian Macaulay refers as "perhaps the most remarkable body of men that the world has ever produced." "That the English people became Protestant," says Bancroft, "is due to the Puritans." And another historian, E.W. Smith, tells us that "the significance of this fact is beyond computation. English Protestantism, with its open Bible, its spiritual and intellectual freedom, meant the Protestantism not only of the American colonies, but of the virile and multiplying race which for three centuries has been carrying the Anglo-Saxon language, religion, and institutions into all the world."

Cromwell, the great Puritan leader and commoner, planted himself on the solid rock of Scripture, and called to himself soldiers who had also planted themselves upon that same rock. The result was an army that for purity and heroism surpassed anything that the world had ever seen. Let us not forget that it was that army that overthrew Catholicism and secured our Protestant heritage. Professor John Fiske, whom some have ranked as one of the outstanding American historians, says, "It is not too much to say that in the seventeenth century the entire political future of mankind was staked on the questions that were at issue in England. Had it not been for the Puritans, political liberty probably would have disappeared from the world. If ever there were men who laid down their lives in the cause of mankind, they were those grim old Ironsides, whose watch-words were texts of Holy Writ, and whose battle-cries were hymns of praise."

And a century before Cromwell's time there had been another great deliverance in English history. In 1588 the Spanish Armada set sail for the conquest of England. Though the pope had blessed the Armada, God blessed and saved Protestant England, and determined the course of history.

In the struggle that freed the Netherlands from the dominating power of the papacy and from the cruel yoke of Spain, we have another glorious chapter in the history of humanity. The tortures of the Spanish Inquisition were applied there as in few other places. That bloodthirsty monster, the duke of Alva, boasted that within the short space of five years he had delivered 18,600 heretics to the executioner.

Says the historian Motley, "The number of Netherlanders that were burned, strangled, beheaded or buried alive, in obedience to the edict of Charles V of Spain, and for the offense of reading the Scriptures, or looking askance at a graven image, or ridiculing the actual presence of the body and blood of Christ in a wafer, have been placed as high as one hundred thousand by distinguished authorities, and have never been put at a lower mark than fifty thousand." During that memorable struggle of eighty years, the Spaniards put more Protestants to death for their conscientious belief than the number of Christians who suffered martyrdom under the Roman emperors in the first three centuries of the Christian era. For nearly three generations Spain, the strongest nation in Europe at that time, labored to stamp out Protestantism and political liberty in those Calvinistic Netherlands, but failed. Because the Protestants sought to worship God according to the dictates of their conscience and not under the galling chains of a corrupt priesthood, their country was invaded and the people subjected to the cruelest tortures the Spaniards could invent. And if it be asked who effected the deliverance, the answer is, it was the Calvinistic prince of Orange, known in history as William the Silent, together with those who held the same creed. Abraham Kuyper, statesman and theologian in Holland, wrote, "If the power of Spain at that time had not been broken by the heroism of the Calvinistic spirit, the history of the Netherlands, of Europe, and of the world would have been as painfully sad and dark as now, thanks to Calvinism, it is bright and inspiring."

Our distinctive American liberties, which came to us through the founding of this republic, also were purchased only through struggle and sacrifice. Two-thirds of the three million inhabitants of our country at the time of the American Revolution were of English Puritan, Scotch Presbyterian, or German or Dutch Reformed stock, and the American independence was secured largely through their willingness to sacrifice life and property if need be. The opening of the revolutionary struggle found the Puritans, Presbyterians, and Reformed ministers and churches lined up solidly on the side of the colonists, and Bancroft credits the Presbyterians with having made the first bold move toward independence. The synod that assembled in Philadelphia in 1775 was the first religious body to declare openly and publicly for independence. It urged the people under its jurisdiction to leave nothing undone that would promote the end in view, and called upon them to pray for the Congress that was then in session. At the time of the American Revolution the Roman Catholics in this country constituted only about one percent of the population. The basic principles on which this nation grew to greatness and through which it has surpassed all of the other nations of the world, and through which it has given our people the highest standard of living in the world, was that of a free church in a free state. Today large numbers of people in the Roman Catholic countries want to migrate to this Protestant United States, just as people in the Communist countries want to migrate here. Practically none want to go the other way. Surely that speaks volumes for the wisdom of our colonial forefathers in founding this nation.

7

War Caused by Sin

"Whence come wars and whence come fightings among you? Come they not hence, even of your pleasures that war in your members? Ye lust and have not: ye kill, and covet, and cannot obtain: ye fight and war; ye have not, because ye ask not." In these words James (4:1, 2) gives us the divine appraisal of human nature, and the real causes of wars. Lust, covetousness, inordinate love of pleasure, and the friendship of the world, he says, are enmity with God.

In an ideal world there would be no sin, and therefore no war. But we do not live in an ideal world. We are living in a world of deep unrest, a world into which sin has entered with devastating effect. Although it is not popular doctrine today, and although we have not space here to elaborate the doctrine, the Scriptures teach clearly and repeatedly that we are members of a fallen race. They teach that as a result of Adam's sin every person born into this world enters it not in a normal but in an abnormal spiritual condition, and that the primary cause of quarrels between individuals and wars between nations is unregenerate, sinful human nature. So long as men's hearts are filled with sin it is vain to expect them to live together in peace and harmony. War is only the outward symptom of a disease that is much more deep-seated. And while we rightly do all in our power to treat the symptom, it is vain to expect any real or permanent cure until the disease itself has been brought under control. God does not prohibit war because He does not prohibit the consequences of sin. War is not an isolated and separate spiritual or religious problem, but merely a part of the much greater and more central problem of sin.

Most pacifists ignore completely the Scripture teaching that we enter this world members of a fallen race. They assume rather that human nature is inherently good. They stress their broad doctrine of "the fatherhood of God and the brotherhood of men," ignoring that not the whole human race as such, but only those who have been regenerated by the supernatural power of the Holy Spirit are truly children of God. "Except one be born anew [born from above], he cannot see the kingdom of God," said Jesus (John 3:3). "As many as received him, to them gave he the right to become children of God, even to them that believe on his name: who are born, not of blood, nor of the will of the flesh, nor of the will of man, but of God" (John 1:12, 13). Jesus declared that the Pharisees were not the children of God but of the devil (John 8:44)—that is, as judged by their inner governing nature they were not righteous and holy like God, but fallen and sinful like the devil, and therefore properly to be called his children. There is, of course, a broad sense in which God as the Creator of all men is said to be the Father of all men. But man by his fall into sin lost his estate of innocence and purity, and came to be actuated by a nature similar to that possessed by the devil, who also is a fallen creature. This does not mean that fallen men are presently as bad as is the devil, but that in principle they are possessed of the same kind of spiritual nature, and that if not hindered by material or social restraints they tend to become worse and worse. So often we hear it said that war is caused by unsound economic or social conditions, and of course those usually are the immediate and outward causes. But how anyone professing to take his religion from the Bible can make a survey of the causes leading to war and totally overlook the fundamental cause, sinful human nature, is beyond logical explanation.

It is to be acknowledged that in the arguments and attitudes of the pacifists there is usually a fine idealism, a noble purpose, a sincere desire to establish world peace. But also in every plan suggested by the peace marchers or the ban-the-bomb crowd there has been a fatal lack, a vitiating principle, which dooms the program to defeat. Almost invariably human depravity is the element that is not given sufficient consideration. That is the fatal defect that wrecks hopes and makes false prophets of those who put their reliance on social improvement, education, the United Nations, World Courts, etc. We certainly do not mean to imply that those things are not good in themselves if properly managed. But we do want to point out that until the hearts of men are changed, the uplift that comes from improved social and political conditions can be but temporary. At no time in history had those things been so aggressively furthered, nor was pacifist sentiment more widespread and articulate as during the twenty-year period that preceded the outbreak of the Second World War; and yet they failed to prevent the development of huge military machines and the mass psychology in several nations that led straight into that war. The initial step in the direction of sensible disarmament and world peace is for individuals and nations to accept the principles that are set forth in Holy Scripture. To put disarmament before moral and spiritual disarmament is to act foolishly and to leave civilization at the mercy of barbaric and beastly impulses.

To state the case in other words, we can say that the underlying fallacy of the whole pacifist movement is that it places *reform* before *redemption,* or even attempts reform without redemption. War is a result of sin, and until the world reaches a higher state spiritually and morally there must continue to be wars, tumults, riots, and bloodshed. These are the natural fruits of sin. Christ did not come primarily as a Reformer, but as a Redeemer. His *first* objective was not the abolishment of slavery, or war, or political oppression, or poverty, but the inward change in the hearts of men, which in due time would automatically destroy all of those evils. In order to be effective and permanent, reform must *follow* redemption. It cannot precede redemption, for it is produced by a power that no man has of himself, a power that God gives only to those who truly accept His Son Jesus Christ as the only Savior from sin.

What folly it is, then, for the church to neglect her real, God-given mission, which is that of delivering souls from the bondage of sin through the preaching of faith in Christ and His finished work, and to embark on programs calling for the reformation of the world through national disarmament and kindred social and political movements. While those things are good in their place, they are, nevertheless, only external and mechanical so far as the real needs of man are concerned. Permanent peace can be ushered in only on a spiritual basis. We are for peace, but not for peace with the devil. Man's real trouble is not external but internal, and until his heart is changed, wars—or their equivalent in individual crimes, which, because they are continuous and widespread, may be fully as bad—will continue to curse the world in spite of all the pacifist programs that can be invented. Our task in the church is to set forth the way of truth and righteousness, and to support the authority of the state in the preservation of peace and security throughout the nation.

8

Military and Police Force Based on the Same Principle

No one would advocate abolishing the police protection in our cities and towns. To do so would place life and property in the hands of lawless gangs. Note, for instance, the suddenness with which looting starts in any community when police protection is lacking, particularly after floods, tornadoes, or earthquakes. The reason we as individuals do not have to carry weapons for self-defense is because we have police to carry them for us. The work of the soldier, like that of the policeman, is not primarily that of killing, but of keeping others from killing. Military and police protection alike are based on physical force, and a moment's reflection should convince us that the arguments of the pacifists, if logically carried out, would as effectively abolish every policeman from our streets as they would abolish our army and navy. That this is often denied does not alter the facts.

Our battle against crime goes on year after year. We insist that the use of armed force is exactly the same in principle whether by the police to stop criminals, or by a nation to stop another nation that is actuated by criminal motives. We are in fact fighting this army of criminals all the time.

And it is as clear as any lesson from history that nations are sometimes actuated by criminal motives, and that they commit murder and robbery on a national scale. In our advanced twentieth century we have seen great military nations, unrestrained by any regard for morality or international justice, arm themselves to the teeth and proceed to the conquest of their weaker neighbors. It is as important nationally to protect our country as it is locally to protect our homes. There are two primary reasons that the United States, despite all of her great wealth and natural resources, has not been made the victim of such attacks as have been other nations that were already overpopulated and comparatively poor: (1) America's very favorable geographical location, and (2) her recognized ability to defend herself. Let no one think that we have escaped for so long for any other reasons.

Right here it will be found worthwhile to listen to one of the most profound thinkers that the church have produced, one whose solid theology and practical wisdom have been all too much neglected by the church in these latter days, John Calvin:

> Now, as it is sometimes necessary for kings and nations to take up arms for the infliction of public justice [i.e., the punishment of criminals], the same reason will lead us to infer the lawfulness of wars which are undertaken for this end. For if they have been entrusted with power to preserve the tranquility of their own territories, to suppress the seditious tumults of disturbers, to succor the victims of oppression, and to punish crimes—can they exert this power for a better purpose than to repel the violence of him who disturbs both the private repose of individuals and the general tranquility of the nations, who incites insurrections, and perpe-

trates acts of oppression, cruelty and every species of crime? And if they justly punish those robbers, whose injuries have only extended to a few persons, shall they suffer a whole district to be plundered and devastated with impunity? For there is no difference whether he, who in a hostile manner invades, disturbs, and plunders the territory of another to which he has no right, be he a king or one of the meanest of mankind: all persons of this description are equally to be considered robbers, and ought to be punished as such. It is the dictate of natural equity, and of the nature of the office, therefore, that princes are armed, not only to restrain the crimes of private individuals by judicial punishments, but also to defend the territories committed to their charge by going to war against any hostile aggression; and the Holy Spirit, in many passages in Scripture, declares that such wars are lawful (*Institutes* IV. xx).

War is justifiable, of course, only when all honorable efforts to avoid it have failed. But when a nation is invaded, its people killed or threatened with slavery worse than death, and property destroyed, it has no alternative but to resist—by any means and at any cost. To fail to resist under such conditions is both immoral and un-Christian. The priceless principles of religious and civil liberty for ourselves and for those who come after us are more important than life itself. Quite plainly there are some things worse than war. To become slaves in body and soul is worse than death. Such existence is in fact a form of living death. Today we need only think of some of the conquered people who are under the godless Russian Communism, or of countries of southeast Asia—Vietnam, Cambodia, and Laos. The nation or the individual who adopts a policy of peace at any price soon finds that there are others who are ready to take unfair advantage. As passionately as we desire peace, there is a point at which the creed of pacifism breaks down and brings worse evils than those it seeks to avoid.

9

America Not a Militaristic Nation

We have defined a militarist as one who favors heavy armaments primarily for purposes of aggression against other nations. Judged by that definition America is not and never has been a militaristic nation. A historical survey of our national policies shows that we have aimed to be neither militaristic nor pacifist. We have never had a militarist president, general of armies, or leading statesmen, such as Napoleon, Hitler, Mussolini, Stalin, or Tojo. Our most illustrious military leaders—Washington, Grant, Lee, Pershing, MacArthur, and Eisenhower—have advocated only such military forces as were necessary to protect the orderly existence of the nation.

In this connection it is of special interest to note that shortly before the outbreak of the Second World War our standing army numbered only 187,000 men and officers, our navy 116,000, and the marines 19,000, a total of only 322,000 (United States Information Service, Washington,

D.C.). That means that, at that time, only about one-fourth of one percent of our population was in the military service of the country, which, incidentally, was also about the same proportion as existed between the police and the civilian population. In all other great countries the ratio was from ten to fifty times as great. In actual size our total forces were exceeded by those of fifteen other nations, although in population we were exceeded only by China, India, and Russia. Figures like these show clearly that the United States is not a militaristic nation and that she desires to live in peace with other nations.

We have seen that the services rendered by the army and navy nationally are very similar to and just as necessary as that which the police render locally. We believe that the United States should have an army and navy sufficient to insure national peace and security, and certainly the world situation that has existed since the Second World War makes it necessary that we have a considerably increased military effectiveness. The present tragic plight of several European nations shows what can happen to an unprepared nation, even though it be a great one. We must never allow our nation to sink into a state of unpreparedness.

There is much wisdom in the advice given by George Washington: "To be prepared for war is one of the most effectual means of preserving peace." Washington was neither a militarist nor a pacifist, but a clear-minded realist, and his words are as true today as when he spoke them. A nation cannot be armed in a day. Experience shows that years of careful planning and training are required to put a nation on a wartime basis, and that is particularly true in our day when so much of our equipment requires highly trained men to operate it.

Within reasonable limits we should be prepared at all times to do our duty in helping to preserve peace among other nations. Occupying the position that we do among the nations, we have a very definite responsibility for the preservation of world civilization. The events of the last few years have made us realize as never before that we are living in a closely knit world, and that what affects one nation for good or evil sooner or later affects all the others. As long as we remain a first-rate nation, we cannot isolate ourselves from the rest of the world. When we see our neighbor's house entered by bandits intent on burning it and killing his family, we are not justified in sitting idly by and doing nothing. We have a God-given position of power and influence among the nations, and that sometimes means that we must act or help act as policeman in maintaining peace and justice. We cannot escape that duty even if we wish. We have performed that duty numerous times in the past, and almost invariably with proper reserve.

Our established national policy has been one of peace with all nations. We were drawn into the First and Second World Wars and into the Korean and Vietnam Wars with great reluctance, and we may be sure that in the future we will not be drawn into any war unless compelled to resist aggression of another nation. Past experience justifies us in saying that American preparedness for war is the best guarantee for peace. This is not militarism or sword-rattling, but a necessary precaution for the protection of a free people. We believe that we are justified in saying that the United States, despite her faults, is the most progressive, the most unselfish, and the most Christian nation in the world, and that with her vast natural resources and her great industrial capacity she is peculiarly fitted—we may even say providentially appointed—to be a strong uplifting, guiding, and stabilizing influence throughout the world.

10

Not to Obey
the Government Blindly

We have said that under normal conditions it is the duty of every loyal citizen to obey his government and to serve in the armed forces of his country if called. We must make it clear, however, that such service is not to be rendered blindly or mechanically. God alone is Lord of the conscience. Our first loyalty is to Him, and we cannot transfer that loyalty to any group of officials, no matter how sincere their intentions.

In this day of abundant newspaper, radio, and TV news reports it is the duty of every citizen, particularly of every Christian citizen, to keep himself intelligently informed concerning national and world events. Particularly in times of national crisis the person who knows himself to be liable for military service should take it upon himself to become a real student of events so that he may act intelligently.

If, however, because of the complexity of causes, the citizen is not able to determine whether or not the war is just, he should obey the order from his government just as he would obey an order from the court in civil affairs, realizing that as a private citizen he may not be in possession of all the important facts. He must remember that the right of judgment concerning war has been committed of God to the government in much the same way that the right of judgment concerning accused persons is committed to the courts. Within all reasonable limits the government, like the courts, should be given the benefit of the doubt. In such cases the citizen is to assume that the lawful rulers of the country, with their wider experience and their more detailed or confidential information, have decided wisely. Particularly in times of national crisis the citizen is to obey the government's orders, not merely when he can find clear scriptural grounds for the things commanded, but regularly unless he can find a scriptural command or principle sufficiently clear to justify his refusal. As Dr. Clarence Bouma has pointed out, "The duty to obey the government is one of the basic duties of all Christian social ethics. The solemn teaching on this score of Paul in Romans 13 is plain. A state in which the citizen obeys the government only when it suits his convenience is no state and that government is no government."

If, however, the citizen is convinced that the particular war into which his country is about to enter is morally wrong, it becomes his duty to protest to the proper authorities. When the government commands the citizen to do something that God has forbidden, or to refrain from doing something that God has commanded, the government has then stepped out of its lawful sphere, and it is his right and duty to disobey such a command. When the early disciples were commanded by the rulers not to preach or teach in the name of Jesus, they flatly refused to obey, saying, "Whether it be right in the sight of God to hearken unto you rather than unto God, judge ye: for we cannot but speak the things which we saw and heard." When in various European countries Protestant believers refused to deny their faith at the command of Roman Catholic rulers, even willingly suffering persecution or martyrdom, they did a highly meritorious thing, and today we honor them as heroes of the faith. If we should be commanded to give up our Christian faith, as has happened in so many Communist countries, or to blaspheme the name of God, or to live an immoral life, it would be our duty to disobey such a command. For in such cases the ruler would have exceeded his lawful authority.

11

Pacifist Pledges

At the opposite extreme from obeying the government blindly are those pacifist campaigns that sometimes are promoted on college and university campuses and in youth conferences in which a false idealism is set before our young people. Many have been persuaded to sign pledges in which they renounce war and pledge themselves never to support or sanction another war regardless of the apparent causes. What blind folly to make such a pledge when there is no way of knowing what the issues may be if the country is called to war! Such pledges are not only treasonable, but unscriptural and un-Christian. And instead of ushering in an era of peace as may be intended, they have just the opposite effect in that they tend to leave the country unprepared and thus actually invite aggression.

Sometimes young people are asked to sign a pledge that they will never "participate" in war, giving the impression that it is an open choice, just as they may choose to participate or not participate in football, or basketball, or any other sport. Let us not be misled by such false propaganda.

To make the case specific, since highly militarized Russia has shown repeatedly that she is ready to resort to brute force and terrorism when that serves her purpose, it ill becomes anyone to pledge himself never to fight for his country, even in self-defense. We have been through this before. For years before the outbreak of the Second World War, the democracies pursued a policy of "appeasement" in their relations with the dictator nations of that day, hoping that each new concession would satisfy the aggressors. But that policy did not lead to peace. It led only to a series of disasters.

It is an easy thing for young people to fall under the spell of pacifist propaganda on a college campus, or in a summer conference, or in a peaceful church in a well-policed city. But let us face those issues in the light of actual happenings in the world about us, and the solution will not appear so easy. We are under no illusions that it is a dreadful thing to be engaged in mortal combat with another human being or with another army. But under circumstances that sometimes occur, not only is such combat sanctioned by God, but it is our duty to perform it with all available resources. Conditions may arise in which it becomes our Christian duty to fight or wage war, as under other conditions it is our Christian duty not to fight or wage war. In times of unrest or of threatened aggression, it is nothing less than criminal to fail to provide our nation with an adequate defense.

And if it is foolish and treasonable for individuals to take pacifist pledges, how much more foolish and treasonable and un-Christian it is for church councils to pledge whole denominations to such a course! We believe that the church and the state have their separate spheres. And on that premise it certainly is not the function of any denomination,

or of the National Council of Churches or the World Council
of Churches to attempt to pre-judge and decide policies of
government. Political pronouncements, and particularly
those having to do with the defense of the country, should
be left to clear-thinking government officials whose special
study is world conditions and trends and who have confidential information the private citizen does not have. There
are few things that can more quickly bring the good name of
the church into justified disrepute than for her to presume
to dictate in matters that are outside her lawful sphere. She
has the right and the duty to speak concerning things that
are morally right or wrong, but her pronouncements concerning things that are primarily political and economic
have too often proved to be shortsighted, impractical, or
even dangerous. Let her beware lest she be led into any
position that involves repudiation of the teachings of Scripture or treason to the nation. Her immediate duty is not the
obstruction of the necessary functions of civil government
through the instillation of a pacifist psychology in the
minds of the people, nor is it a campaign to limit our military
effectiveness, but the promotion of the only permanently
constructive policy of peace, the presentation of the
gospel of redemption to individual souls. As individuals are
changed, the nations will be changed, and the causes that
lead to war will fade away. There is no other way.

12

Conscientious Objectors

Closely related to the problem of pacifist pledges is that of conscientious objectors. It would seem to be self-evident that when one's country needs to be defended in order to prevent aggression, every able-bodied man is under obligation to contribute toward that defense in the capacity in which he is best fitted. That will mean military service for some and support of various kinds for others, the government being the arbitrator as to the capacity in which each person shall serve. Surely every person who has enjoyed or expects to enjoy the blessings and privileges of life in a particular country is under obligation to assist in the defense of that country.

Too often conscientious objections have been pleaded merely as a cloak for cowardice. If, however, the objector is sincere, as indeed some are, he can at least be given supporting work of some kind after due inquiry has been made to establish his sincerity. That has been the practice followed by the United States. And yet in regard to our school system, we make no such exceptions in behalf of those who do not want to educate their children, although we do permit private schools and sometimes home schooling to supply that need. Nor do we excuse anyone from the duty of paying taxes merely because he may be opposed to our form of government or to the particular purpose for which the tax money is spent. Nor is such practice considered unreasonable. But because of the personal element involved it is acknowledged that one who is conscientiously opposed to military service probably would not make a good soldier and had better be assigned to some other work. The first step Gideon took in preparing his army for battle was to get rid of those who were unwilling; then he ridded himself of the inefficient. We do not admit the conscientious objector's claim to be valid, for the simple reason that it is based on a false premise. But only in case he refuses to aid his country in this more limited capacity should he be subject to punishment.

During the First World War many of the conscientious objectors in England who were Quakers proved their sincerity and their loyalty by volunteering to man the mine sweepers, a work that they knew quite well would expose them to more danger than would regular army or navy service. We respect the courage and sincerity of such men even though we do not agree with their reasoning.

In this regard it should be remembered that not the individual conscience but the full system of doctrine as taught in the Scriptures is the final authority for both faith and practice. Individual statements in the Bible are sometimes taken out of context and used to support false positions. But the Bible is not self-contradictory. It contains one unified system of truth, all parts of which, if taken in their true context and properly understood, are consistent with all other parts. And in that system war is authorized under certain conditions. When we find a person whose conscience disapproves of something that the Bible approves, we may be sure that he has been misled. God has ordained civil governments and has commanded that His children shall render lawful obedience to them. To those governments has been given the duty locally and nationally to preserve law and order, even though in order to do so, they sometimes have to resort to force.

Sincere Christians often differ in their judgments as to what things are right and what are wrong, such as smoking, dancing, theater attendance, Sunday observance, or the amount of money they should spend on luxuries. Given a particular background, the individual's moral judgment decides whether any particular action is right or wrong for him. Then after he has acted or has refrained from acting, his conscience tells him whether he as an individual and in those particular circumstances did right or wrong. Because of a perversion of the moral judgment, conscience does not tell the Christian Scientist that he has done wrong when he refuses to call a doctor for himself or for a member of his family who is sick; nor does it tell a Mormon that he is doing wrong when he practices polygamy. Conscience is infallible only in the realm of moral intention. But neither the moral judgment nor the conscience is infallible as to what is ultimately right or wrong. To find that out we must go to the Bible.

13

Modern Pacifism Allied with Radicalism

Another prominent feature of the modern pacifist movement to which we strenuously object is its leadership, particularly in the political and interdenominational spheres. While there are many sincere Christians connected with it, an unduly large proportion of its leaders have come from the ranks of church liberals, socialists, secular humanists, atheists, and Communists—the type of people with whom it is extremely dangerous to mingle. Those various groups find it possible to work together on a humanistic basis. While the Christian pacifist wants disarmament for one reason, the Communist wants it for an entirely different reason; and yet the effect of their influence is the same—a defenseless America. The Christian pacifist desires disarmament because he believes that if war is made impossible, man's nobler nature will assert itself and ultimately develop an ideal society. The Communist desires disarmament and promotes a peace-at-any-price psychology in the hope that eventually the time will come when his system can be more easily imposed on an unsuspecting people. Each advocates it for the United States, even unilateral disarmament, without any guarantee that there will also be disarmament on the part of other nations, particularly on the part of highly militarized Russia.

Often without realizing it or intending it, the Christian pacifist is found working hand in glove with radicals whose ultimate purposes are quite different from his. But what a bitter experience it might turn out to be for the person who sincerely desires peace to discover that the system which he helped to promote actually had the opposite effect! Although sincere in his purpose, he surely has strange bedfellows. And are we not told that in some respects the sons of this world are for their own generation wiser than the sons of light (Luke 16:8)?

Almost invariably the Christian pacifist turns out to be a liberal in the church. He laughs at the Christian doctrine of the sovereignty of God and the sinfulness of man; and, believing that human nature is essentially good and needs only to be properly directed, he thinks that man by his own efforts is working himself to a higher level of religion and morality. Actuated by those assumptions, he repudiates the divine Christ, reduces Him to a mere moral teacher and good example, and denies or ignores the consequences of sin. He calls for a shorter Bible and expects the kingdom of God to be established on earth largely through such things as social legislation, education, and disarmament.

The testimony of history is very clear to the effect that true Christianity tends to develop brave, courageous men with strong convictions for the right. Never does it produce cowards. True religion and true patriotism have always gone hand in hand, while unbelief, doubt, and liberalism have invariably been accompanied by socialism, Communism, radicalism, and other enemies of free government.

Not long ago one of our church magazines had occasion to give this warning on its editorial page: "Conservative and patriotic laymen have much fault to find with the radical ministers who are fairly common in the Protestant communions. One described them as 'preachers who have abandoned the Gospel of salvation for the Social Gospel; the Bible for the writings of "Saint" Karl Marx, and who wave the red flag in times of peace and the white flag in times of war.' The fact has often been pointed out that the social radical is always a modernist in theology."

And in a prominent article in another church magazine, we find these words:

> It is a fact that most of the outstanding pacifist leaders of America and Europe today are men who have broken with evangelical Christianity, men who frankly deny most, or all of the great fundamental beliefs of Christians. The leadership of these men, so much a unit in their pacifist teachings, is a type of leadership evangelical Christians should watch carefully. My one desire is to flee from such men and their leadership. But if a man identifies himself with the present pacifist movement he finds that type on every side and in the lead. This alone should provoke thought and bring pause.

It is not only interesting but highly instructive to observe the course liberalism has followed. It is a matter of historical record that liberalism ("Higher Criticism" as it was first called, or "Destructive Criticism" as it might more appropriately have been called) was born in Germany about 150 years ago. With characteristic German thoroughness and efficiency, the scholars set to work to study and analyze the Bible. But as time went on that study came to be conducted less and less from the viewpoint of evangelical Christianity, and more and more from that of humanistic philosophy and skepticism. Although many of the old terms were retained, faith in the Bible as a divinely inspired book was destroyed, theology as a science was practically discarded, and man's origin was ascribed to an evolutionary process rather than to a creative act of God. Human conduct came to be based more and more on what was considered expedient or practical than on a supernaturally given moral code, and in general a broad system of humanitarianism or self-salvation was substituted for the gospel of redemption through Christ. The general tendency and influence of the movement was far more atheistic than was realized at the time.

While the movement arose in Germany, it did not stay there, but spread to France, Holland, England, and America, and with the same results. The situation was analyzed briefly and accurately by an American writer as follows:

> Luther gave Germany the Bible in her own tongue and made her the great people which she later became, many of her emigrants becoming our finest citizens and homemakers. Then her universities began turning out a subtile learning which blasted the very foundations on which she stood. The Bible which Luther gave her, and with it her faith, was ploughed under. The soil was then left ready for any sowing, and the seed which fell upon it was Nietzsche's philosophy. This became the new philosophy of a generation that knew not Joseph, the philosophy of Nazism—that might makes right and that Christianity is wrong. That let loose on the face of the earth a scourge with demonical aim to crush all minorities and liberties and the determination to rule or die. Of course in saying these things we know there are always individual exceptions, and in all of this we are speaking in a general summary. Through the years Germany has produced some of the finest Christians that ever lived (Dr. George W. Arms).

14

Compulsory Military Training

In times of national crisis, when defense becomes imperative, the property, services, and even the lives of the citizens must in principle be placed at the service of the nation. Under such conditions the peacetime limitations that make it possible to give or to withhold no longer apply. Every able-bodied man is under obligation to serve in the capacity in which he can be most effective. Despite the dislike that the American people have for compulsion in any sphere, they demand that we shall have an adequate national defense in order that the terrible price that some other nations have had to pay may not be exacted of us. Particularly when the world is in such an unstable state as now exists, surely the fairest, surest, and most efficient way to secure that defense is through compulsory military training. It will do but little good to build large numbers of planes, missiles, ships, and tanks if we do not have men trained to operate them. Modern war moves so swiftly that it is not possible to provide that training after the fighting has begun. It is nothing short of criminal for a nation to send its soldiers into battle unprepared. Unless the service is made universal and compulsory, only the best and bravest young men are killed or disabled in large numbers, while the selfish and spiritually weak remain at home to perpetuate the race.

Let no one say that this proposal runs counter to our principle of national freedom. It is in fact of the very essence of a free society that when the privileges and opportunities are shared by all alike, the obligations and responsibilities of defending that society must be shared by all alike. No one has the right to enjoy the blessings of religious and civil freedom unless he, together with all other free men, is willing to defend that freedom.

Furthermore, and more important, a free state, in order to remain free, must be served by a citizen army. Experience shows quite clearly that an army can be kept democratic only if it is based on short-term universal service, say, one or two years, rather than on long-term service of professional soldiers. The tendency is for the long-term professional army to feel that it alone is the protector of the state, to identify its existence with the existence of the state, and thus to become a state within a state. That is the kind of militarism that leads to military dictatorship and loss of the people's liberties. In order that the army shall not rule the state, it must be of the same composition as the state, that is, composed of free citizens. How often we have seen small army groups take over governments, particularly in Latin America! It is a matter of historical record that Hitler was a creation of the long-term professional army in Germany. In order to prevent the training of large numbers of German soldiers, the Treaty of Versailles at the close of the First World War prohibited short-term military service and required 12 years' service of every soldier. The inevitable result was that the army became a professional body. Had the German republic been served by an army composed of citizens organized to defend a free state, there is every reason to believe that it would have endured. But instead the treaty created a professional army, which, while composed of comparatively few soldiers, soon developed into a state within the state, an army that set itself to nullify the Treaty of Versailles and to regain its former power. That army gave Hitler his first platform, employed him as its speaker, and subsidized his newspaper. With the aid of that army he overthrew the Weimar Republic and established himself as the prime minister.

The relation that exists between a free people and short-term universal military training was clearly expressed by Dorothy Thompson, a political analyst who wrote during the Second World War period:

> The only form of military defense that is not a menace to democracy is that built upon universal military service. The oldest and, for its size, the strongest democracy in the world today is the Swiss. Like our own, it was founded not on nationality but upon an idea; it came into being with an oath—the oath to be free and to defend that freedom. It is and has been a democracy in which every citizen is a soldier and every soldier is a citizen. And it has thus avoided militarism while being, for its size, so strong that its powerful neighbors prefer to touch any other small state rather than the porcupine of Switzerland. An army based on universal service cannot become a STATE *within* a State, because its social frontiers are coincident with the frontiers of the State. An army of democratic citizens is a democratic army.

One very important historical principle that has always been incorporated in American draft laws is that which provided that in all cases those chosen for military service should be chosen by local civilian boards, and that no one already in the army or navy could serve on those boards. It was not the army that reached out and took a man from civil life, but a local civilian board that sent the man to the army. After an examination of all the circumstances of the eligible men of the community, the board, composed of the man's own neighbors, designated him as the one chosen to go and fight for them. If the man so designated felt that he had not been chosen fairly, he had the privilege of laying his case before an appeal board, also composed of civilians. Through the whole process the choices were made by civilians who designated certain men to serve them in the army. Also in accord with this, American tradition requires that the Secretary of Defense in the President's cabinet shall be a civilian. All of this assures the subordination of the military to the body politic, and thus preserves one of the basic principles of representative government. Our nation is a republic, that is, a nation governed by representatives duly elected by the people.

Nor is conscription in itself contrary to our traditional American ideals. Rather it is an old and accepted principle and has been resorted to repeatedly when danger has threatened. Its roots were in the old Common Law. In colonial days every free man was considered under obligation to provide his own arms and to assist in the common defense. Washington urged it as the only effective method to win the Revolutionary War, and at the time of the adoption of the Federal Constitution, provision for universal service was made in the basic laws of nine of the thirteen states. It was used during the War of 1812, by both sides during the Civil War, and in both the First and Second World Wars. It is our acknowledged method of raising an army when danger threatens. In times of national crisis the nation's maximum manpower can no more be obtained by voluntary enlistments without conscription than the cost of the war can be met by voluntary contributions without compulsory taxation. And in the final analysis the one is just as fair as is the other.

The American conscription plan that was used during the Second World War was unique only in so far as that was the first time that conscription was authorized before we became involved in the war. The need for conscription had become apparent. Wars are now fought without waiting for a declaration of war. And for several years some powerful nations had been at war with our form of government, our free institutions, and our way of life. With the advent of missiles, airplanes, tanks, and other modern instruments, wars are fought with lightning speed. There is no time to prepare after the war starts.

We do not mean to imply that military training is a pleasant experience, for usually it is not. Usually it means hard work and is undertaken at considerable inconvenience. But in addition to the security that it provides for the nation as a whole, there are also certain benefits that accrue to the individual soldier. Among these are a deeper sense of national responsibility and patriotism, improved posture, respect for constituted authority, the inspiration that comes from working in close cooperation with a great body of other men in behalf of a worthy cause, the opportunity to travel, a broadened outlook on life, and by no means least, the mastery of a trade if one is assigned to a special work.

We submit further that, in the first place, no nation is safe unless her citizens are trained to defend her, and that, in the second place, the man who, in addition to his regular occupation, is also trained to defend his country is a more valuable citizen and will be more honored in his home and in his community than one who is not so trained.

15

War as a Judgment on Nations

We often hear the expression "the Christian nations." Strictly speaking, there is not so much as one truly Christian nation anywhere in the world, and there never has been. While in a number of nations Christian standards are outwardly acknowledged as the rule by which behavior should be regulated, it cannot be said that in any one a majority of the people accept Christ as their Savior and serve God consistently. The nations of Europe and of North and South America are Christian only in the sense that Christianity rather than Buddhism or Mohammedanism or some other is the preferred religion. All of these, including the United States, at various times have proved themselves essentially selfish and indifferent to or openly contemptuous of God's laws.

In order to make these facts clear, let us consider some events that have happened within the lifetime of people still living. We saw Russia set up an aggressively Communistic government and kill literally millions of her own citizens through a deliberately imposed famine when they did not cooperate with that government. We saw Germany crush out the liberties of her own people and ruthlessly seize the territory of numerous neighboring nations. We saw Italy ravage Ethiopia and interfere without cause in the affairs of Spain. We saw England and France and the United States refuse to sell supplies to the legitimate government of Spain when that refusal meant that country would fall victim to Mussolini's and Hitler's mercenary forces, thus consigning Spain to more than thirty years of military fascist dictatorship. We saw the Roman Catholic Church, which claims and exercises temporal as well as spiritual power, pronounce its blessing on the Italian campaigns in Ethiopia and Spain. We have seen numerous nations repudiate their foreign debts and confiscate the property of foreign investors. We have seen the United States through its Supreme Court sanction the murder of millions of unborn babies through its legalizing of abortion. And we have seen the American people spend approximately ten times as much per year on liquor and tobacco as they give to their churches. In so-called Christian America respect for the Bible as the Word of God and respect for His church as a divinely established institution is far short of what it should be.

In the light of such facts need we ask why God permits war? Very evidently He permits it—we may even say that sometimes He sends it—as a judgment on nations. In regard to our own nation, we must acknowledge that it has been only by the mercy of God, and not our own righteousness, that we have been so largely spared the ravages of war. The marvel is, not that God has brought some nations to judgment through war, but that in His mercy He has granted such long periods of peace and has allowed so many nations to escape those horrors for such a long time.

That war was used as a judgment on the nation of Israel is repeatedly stated in the Old Testament. "And the children of Israel did that which was evil in the sight of Jehovah," said the writer of the book of Judges, "and Jehovah delivered them into the hand of Midian seven years" (6:1). "And the children of Israel again did that which was evil in the sight of Jehovah; and Jehovah delivered them into the hands of the Philistines forty years" (Judg. 13:1). Isaiah gave the clear warning: "If ye are willing and obedient, ye shall eat the good of the land: but if ye refuse and rebel, ye shall be devoured with the sword; for the mouth of Jehovah hath spoken it" (1:19, 20). Listen to the words of the Lord as, speaking through the prophet Jeremiah, He calls all people to witness what is about to happen:

> Hear, O earth; behold, I will bring evil upon this people, even the fruit of their thoughts, because they have not hearkened unto my words; and as for my law, they have rejected it. . . . Thus saith Jehovah, Behold, a people cometh from the north country; and a great nation shall be stirred up from the uttermost parts of the earth. They lay hold on bow and spear; they are cruel, and they have no mercy; their voice roareth like the sea, and they ride upon horses, every one set in array, as a man to the battle, against thee, O daughter of Zion (6:19-23).

And a little later we read,

> I have spoken unto you, rising up early and speaking, but ye have not hearkened. . . . Therefore thus saith Jehovah of hosts: Because ye have not heard my words, behold, I will send and take all the families of the north, saith Jehovah, and I will send unto Nebuchadnezzar the king of Babylon, my servant, and will bring them against this land, and against the inhabitants thereof, and against all these nations round about; and I will utterly destroy them, and make them an astonishment, and a hissing, and perpetual desolations. . . . And it shall come to pass, when seventy years are accom-

plished that I will punish the king of Babylon, and that nation, saith Jehovah, for their iniquity, and the land of the Chaldeans: and I will make it desolate for ever (Jer. 25:3-12).

Here we are told that God used the pagan nation of Babylon to punish apostate Israel. He even refers to Nebuchadnezzar as "my servant"—not in the sense that Nebuchadnezzar worshiped the true God or intentionally served Him, for he did not even know that he was being so used, but in the sense that he was the Lord's instrument. In due time he too would be punished for his atrocities.

And in the book of Habakkuk we read,

> Behold ye among the nations, and look, and wonder marvelously, for I am working a work in your days, which ye will not believe though it be told you. For, lo, I raise up the Chaldeans, that bitter and hasty nation, that march through the breadth of the earth, to possess dwelling-places that are not theirs. They are terrible and dreadful; their judgment and their dignity proceed from themselves. Their horses also are swifter than leopards, and are more fierce than the evening wolves; and their horsemen press proudly on: yea, their horsemen come from far; they fly as an eagle that hasteth to devour. They come all of them for violence; the set of their faces is forward; and they gather captives as the sand. Yea, he scoffeth at kings, and princes are a derision unto them; he derideth every stronghold; for he heapeth up dust, and taketh it (1:5-10).

And behind all of this the prophet sees the hand of God: "O Jehovah, thou hast ordained him for judgment: and thou, O Rock, hast established him for correction" (Hab. 1:6-12). Later the Chaldeans in their turn were judged and destroyed for their wickedness.

In Isaiah 10:5-15 we have a very remarkable statement as to the manner in which God sometimes chastises His disobedient people with war, using a great pagan nation for that purpose as easily as a father uses a rod in the chastisement of his son, yet without that nation being aware that it is being so used. And in the same sense that the king of Assyria or the king of Babylon is referred to as God's "servant," some of the ruthless dictators of our day may also be His servants, designed for the correction of other people, as also to be punished in due time for their atrocities.

It will help immensely in the discussion of this problem if we keep in mind the lesson taught so repeatedly in Scripture, that the suffering that God brings upon His wayward people is, strictly speaking, *chastisement*, that is, suffering designed for their reformation; and the suffering that He inflicts upon the wicked is *punishment*, that is, suffering inflicted as the just desert for evil doing and without any thought of reformation. The former is disciplinary and caused the children of Israel to see the folly of their evil ways, thus inclining them to return to God. The latter is punitive and repressive, and resulted eventually in the complete destruction of the Philistines, Egyptians, Assyrians, and others. There was never any question of the children of Israel being worse than the Philistines or the Egyptians or the Assyrians. Despite the Israelites' faults, they were relatively much better than, though often subdued by, the other nations. God in His providential control often uses the worse people to correct the better. And if the sufferings Israel experienced were horrible, let us remember that the sins for which she was to be purged were horrible and that the sufferings were suited to the offense.

In God's Word the conditions on which sufferings will be averted for the land are clearly set forth. "If my people, who are called by my name, shall humble themselves, and pray, and seek my face, and turn from their wicked ways, then will I hear from heaven, and will forgive their sins, and will heal their land" (II Chron. 7:14).

16

Consequences of War Not All Bad

The first and more visible effects of almost every war are bad. War involves the death of some, the crippling of many others, the destruction of property, and the accumulation of debt. But the consequences are not all bad. Many a country has preserved the great majority of its people, its religious and political liberty, and the bulk of its property by a courageous stand against a would-be aggressor. When those are saved, the first cost in life and treasure is not to be considered excessive.

The point needs no elaboration that the consequences that we first think of, the destruction of life and property, are bad. But it must not be forgotten that in times of national emergency, when people realize that their very lives and country are at stake, some virtues assert themselves as at no other time. In such crises multitudes are drawn together with a new sense of patriotism, bravery, self-sacrifice, and duty to others—virtues that often lie dormant in times of peace. We instinctively admire the patriot who if need be is willing to give his life for his country.

One really admirable result that follows the return of militiamen to private life is the promotion that comes to many who have served their country bravely and well. In the past an unduly large proportion of our presidents, senators, governors, college and university presidents, editors, and jurists have been men who had records of distinguished military service and who in turn were honored by the people they had served.

The social leveling process that occurs in military life, when men from all walks of life—rich and poor, country-bred and city-reared, farmer, manual laborer, and white collar worker—learn to live and work side by side, to depend upon each other in the face of danger, and to appreciate each other's dignity as American citizens, is of inestimable value. Nor to be overlooked is the broadening influence that comes through travel and in mingling with other peoples. The classic example of this latter influence is found in Europe during the Middle Ages when the crusades brought Western Europe into fresh contact with the Greek and Hebrew civilizations, which had been largely lost, events that led directly to the Renaissance, which in turn provided the intellectual and cultural background for the Reformation. And the First and Second World Wars brought out a flood of inventions, medical discoveries, and industrial developments that have served valuable purposes in times of peace. We are not saying that those secondary effects offset the first costs of war; far from it. But we are saying that those were good so far as they went.

Sometimes we hear it said that war engenders hatred. It is true that the tendency in the unregenerate heart is strong in that direction, and oftentimes that tendency is aggravated by a lying propaganda carried on by one or both sides. Yet there is no sound reason why defensive warfare should not be carried on without hatred. Although men seek to the utmost of their ability to destroy each other while the battle rages, it is well known that as soon as the battle is over, the enemy wounded are usually taken to hospitals and are given as good care as are the wounded of the victorious army. This is proof that even during the battle the soldiers are not actuated by hatred but by a sense of governmental responsibility and self-preservation. During the Civil War Abraham Lincoln did not hate the people of the South, nor did Robert E. Lee hate the people of the North. There is no more reason why the soldier in his line of official duty should hate those who are in the opposing army than there is that the policeman should hate those whom he must arrest, or the judge hate those whom he must sentence to prison or even to death. That war causes hatred is not so true as that hatred causes war.

It has also been said that war blights the lives of men morally and spiritually. This, again, is at best a half-truth. In the first place, a person does not necessarily escape bad influences by staying out of the army. War has blighted the lives of many. But so has college, so has business, so has politics, and so have the medical and legal professions, for the very simple reason that those things which are good in themselves have been abused.

Concerning this phase of the question, let us listen to one who spoke out of a wealth of experience, a First World War chaplain in the American army, later president of Wheaton College and professor at Covenant Theological Seminary, Dr. J. Oliver Buswell:

> Much has been said of the evil effects upon the character of young men who go into military service. I can say very positively that it is not military service which destroys char-

acter. The trouble with the moral character of young men serving under arms during the World War was simply that so many of them had come from private life, and continued to live as they had lived or wanted to live as civilians.

It is true that young men in the late teens or the early twenties, taken away from home in any cause and suddenly meeting the temptations of the world, undergo a severe test of character. I have seen many fail morally in military life, but I have seen other men greatly strengthened by military experience. The regiment with which I served in France was composed of men of excellent character, above the average of American civilian life. Several of them were ministers, a number were school teachers, many were distinguished men in business or professional life, and many of them were men of Christian character and standing in their home communities. While it is true that many men have fallen into ways which are morally wrong, yet I know personally of many who became Christians and who learned to pray, and who learned to live the Christian life, and who learned to bear difficulties with courageous faith in God, in military service in our regiment. A very large number of our soldiers carried pocket Testaments, and read them faithfully. Our religious services were very well attended. In fact, when circumstances were at all favorable, our church service, Bible classes and other religious activities were better supported than would have been the case among a similar number of men in almost any civilian community. Some of the best religious services, prayer meetings, and testimony meetings that I ever attended in my life were services in the United States Army. . . . We went into the Meuse-Argonne drive with 3,200 men. After four days of terrific fighting we came out with 600 men and twenty-three officers. Officers of the regiment said at the time that those who were known to be Christian men were the most courageous, the most daring, and the most faithful under the terrific strain of those days.

Let us summarize what the attitude of the Christian should be toward the reality of war as found in this world. And then we shall add a chapter regarding the critical situation that faces us today.

We conclude that war is a direct result of the sin and selfishness that resides in the human heart. Of all the plans offered for its cure, there is only one that promises effectively to rid the world of this evil. And that is the program of Christ as presented in the gospel. Only as the Prince of Peace rules in human hearts, and through them in the nations, will there be an end to strife between individuals and to wars between nations. This plan goes to the root of the matter, while all others merely scratch the surface. It attempts to heal the ancient breach between the lion and the lamb, not by teaching the lion good manners, but by changing the lion's nature.

God sent the Son of His love into the world to die for us and to save us. And because men will not see this, but insist on building their superficial idealisms and going their own ways, He permits such a thing as war to chastise and punish them, to teach them what a heinous thing sin is, and to call them to repentance and acceptance of His gracious offer. What men refuse to learn through the preaching of the gospel in times of peace God often reveals to them through the suffering and destruction that comes through war. Hardly any words are found more often in the Old Testament as a description of the children of Israel than these, that "in their trouble and distress they cried unto the Lord."

Although the world has been in possession of Christ's plan of redemption for nearly two thousand years, there is not even yet so much as one nation, great or small, where the rank and file of the people are truly Christian. We are making progress. The church is growing and has spread around the world. And there are tens of millions of true Christians. But their number still is small compared to that of the unbelievers. It certainly is time that we as Christians take our religion seriously and settle down to our task of evangelizing and Christianizing the world.

We believe that we are justified in saying that the greatest hindrance to the progress of Christianity today is not any one of the pagan religions, or any false system of philosophy, or the liquor or drug traffic, or any political system, but *a secular way of life* on the part of many professing Christians. That manner of life often makes it impossible to see anything distinctive in them. And that brings the church into disrepute.

That the plan of Christ does work has been proved repeatedly. In individual after individual, and in community after community, it has worked marvelously. It has never failed where it has been given a fair trial. It has turned defiant sinners into saints, it has turned storm-tossed homes into centers of love and devotion, and it has turned strife-torn communities into peaceable and prosperous havens of rest. Even in the human sphere in this world it works marvels, and in the divine sphere it means the difference between eternal life and eternal death. While the gospel has been preached throughout our American homeland as in no other nation of the world, it has been applied only halfheartedly. When we become aroused to a national peril, we raise an army and transform hundreds of our industrial plants into armor and ammunition factories. What we need in our spiritual realm is an awakened consciousness of our spiritual responsibility such as will transform every home and church and school in the land into a plant for the nurturing of Christian men and women.

17

The Danger We Face

We have had much to say about the general principles of war and peace. Let us now look quite seriously at the actual dangers that face our nation today. Most Americans unfortunately are ill-informed concerning the relative strength of the American and Soviet military forces. In most categories the Soviets are definitely superior in the number of military machines and in the number of men trained to operate those machines. In some categories, or even in most, they outnumber us by two or three to one. And they are constantly increasing the lead.

In 1946 Sir Winston Churchill, the wartime Premier of Great Britain, in a speech at Fulton, Missouri, warned that our former ally, the Soviet Union, had become a mortal danger to the peace and freedom of the world. It had at that time swallowed up all of the countries of Eastern and Southeastern Europe except Greece, and it was threatening to swallow up others. And that was before it had atomic weapons. In the years that have followed, it has become a far more mortal danger. Had Churchill's advice been heeded at that time, we would not be living under the balance of terror that exists today.

Admiral Elmo Zumwalt, former Chief of United States Naval Operations, has said,   "The Soviet goals are quite clear. They intend to achieve political, military and economic hegemony over the world. They intend to use their immense strategic nuclear superiority and their superior armies, navies and air forces to force the West to accommodate to their expansionism in various parts of the globe."

And Alexander Solzhenitsyn, a Russian exile who knows that system through bitter firsthand experience, has said,

> Communism stops only when it encounters a wall, even if it is only a wall of resolve. The West cannot now avoid erecting such a wall in what is already its hour of extremity. Meanwhile, however, 20 possible allies have fallen to Communism since World War II. Meanwhile, Western technology has helped develop the terrifying military power of the Communist world. The wall will have to be erected with what strength remains. The present generation of Westerners will have to take a stand on the road upon which its predecessors have so thoughtlessly retreated for 60 years.

And yet we have people today, in the United States and in Western Europe, who are opposing our military defense program, who are engaged in "peace marches," sometimes violent. Many in Western Europe are protesting against the deployment of nuclear weapons, even though those are for their own protection. We know that much of that unrest is promoted by Russian propaganda. Major Larkin, USA (Ret.), former Deputy Director of the Defense Intelligence Agency, has reported that the KGB is spending $300 million to promote peace movements in the United States and Western Europe, with the purpose of dividing and terrifying our people.

Actually, the Russians do not want nuclear war any more than we do, for they know that that would cause great destruction to their country as well as ours. What they hope to do is to blackmail us and other nations into compliance or surrender, and so get our very productive economic system intact.

But what the Russians apparently fail to understand is that this American free enterprise system, which is based on freedom to invest and to share profits and losses, could not possibly function under Communism, but would immediately collapse. Nevertheless, they have made this proposal, that *if we will promise not to use atomic weapons first,* they are willing to enter into a substantial arms reduction agreement. But that would leave them with enormous infantry and land forces intact. They could then pour conventional weapons into one country after another where it would be impossible for us to match them, and so take over those countries practically at will. The atomic bomb is our protection against such aggression.

After the Second World War, General MacArthur, who in the opinion of the present writer was the greatest military leader this nation has produced, warned that we should never again engage in a land war in Asia. We violated that warning when we went into the Korean and Vietnam Wars, and we paid a fearful price for that folly.

Ever since the Second World War the United States and the Soviet Union have been locked in a long and costly and dangerous rivalry. We hold fundamentally different and irreconcilable views of human existence. The basic principles that have governed American life since we became a nation are set forth in the Declaration of Independence:

> We hold these truths to be self evident, that all men are created equal, that they are endowed by their Creator with certain unalienable Rights, that among these are Life, Liberty

and the pursuit of Happiness. That to secure these rights, Governments are instituted among men, deriving their just powers from the consent of the governed.

Our way of life is one in which the state is subservient to the interests of the people. What we have is properly termed a republic, a system in which we are governed by duly elected representatives, and in which we have a free economic system (generally termed free enterprise), a legal system based on laws that guarantee human rights, freedom of religion, and freedom of expression, which includes the right to criticize our own government.

In contrast with this, the Communists put the affairs of the nation in the hands of a very small, tyrannical group. What actually happened in Russia was that power was seized by a group of anarchists, criminals, Lenin and Trotsky and their followers, who have since governed for their own good, while the people have absolutely no voice in affairs of government.

After the Second World War the United States, governed by its people, did what is normally done after a war: it drastically reduced its defense spending, froze its strategic nuclear forces, reduced its navy to about half its wartime strength, and cut back its conventional land and air forces. But the Soviets did the exact opposite. They maintained their land and air forces, built a strong navy, and developed nuclear power with an explosive yield calculated to be able to destroy the American strategic force on the ground.

As a result of that course of action, the free world is now confronted with a threat to its very survival. The Soviets have achieved military superiority. They probably have twice as many and larger ICBM warheads as we have, three times as many warships and missile submarines, four times as many tanks and artillery, and nearly three million men in their army, with millions more who have had military training. President Reagan is trying hard to build up our forces, but is having strong partisan opposition in Congress. But if we do not restore our defenses, we subject ourselves to Soviet blackmail or all-out war.

The competition between the American and the Soviet systems clearly is permanent and irreconcilable. In the end one must defeat the other. In the words of one Soviet text, "Communists are not willing to make fundamental concessions and are not about to repudiate their belief in the ultimate universal triumph of Communism; they do indeed consider co-existence as something that will not last forever, but only until the day that Capitalism ceases to exist."

The resources and natural wealth of the United States and its allies is probably double that of the Soviet bloc. But thus far we have not understood what our problem is, and we have lacked the unity to use these resources effectively.

How then can the free world successfully oppose the Communist threat? Much the best information that we have found regarding this broad problem is in a 1984 book, *A Strategy for Peace Through Strength*, published by the American Security Council Foundation, based in Boston, Virginia. This book offers the following program:

> A key tool available to the United States in rolling back the Soviet momentum is communications. Chief among these are the radio—Voice of America and Radio Liberty/Radio Free Europe—and satellite television, which can reach into areas barred to other forms of American influence. . . . To date our communications have been among the most effective means of spreading the Western values of freedom and democracy, even with the minimal official encouragement they have received. This should be greatly expanded and focused on certain areas.

> A second means of rolling back the influence of Communism is to describe the shambles its "scientifically planned" econo-

my makes of the lives of its citizens. In every country where Communism has been in control for as much as 20 years the economy is unquestionably in shambles. Merely the existence of well-made Western merchandise is a disrupting influence in the communist systems, which are forced to explain away their own shoddy products. Of more importance is the disruption that "centralized planning" causes in the Soviet Union, where meat is rationed; in Poland, where food is rationed; or in Cuba, where everything is rationed.

The greatest weakness of all in the communist system should be exploited—its denial of freedom to its citizens. Walls have to be built to keep the people within the Soviet system. A person cannot even go from one town to another except he first get permission from the police; and the police in the town to which he goes must be informed of his coming. This fact should be more than enough to totally alienate all nations of the world except for those that have adopted their own form of repression (pp. 74, 75).

The United States and the Western European countries have enormous power that can be applied through our economic system if we will but use it wisely. But ever since the close of the Second World War, we have helped the Soviets avoid the impact of their own inefficiency by sharing with them our technical know-how and extending massive credits and loans—for which we have received no appreciation but only hatred and contempt. Certainly they never would share any of their assets with any capitalistic nation. And surely they must think that we are simply fools when we do so with them. In so many of our dealings with the Communists we have abandoned ordinary common sense. And now we are paying a terrible price for that folly. Surely the best way to accelerate the process of Communist decline is to let that system fall of its own weight.

The following material having to do with the terrible danger that we face in the Caribbean area is taken from the

August 1983 *Washington Report,* of the American Security Council Foundation (quoted by permission):

> Throughout Central America and the Caribbean Basin a series of events is taking place at an accelerating rate which, if unchecked, will bring Communist imperialism to the region and ultimately pose a direct threat to the survival of the United States. The insidious nature of the indirect aggression now going on raises the question of whether the democratic governments of the area can respond effectively to this form of challenge.

Doctrines in Conflict

Although the situation in the Caribbean Basin is complex, several analysts, such as Stan Evans and George Will, have noted that the conflict is between two basic doctrines: The Monroe Doctrine, presented by President James Monroe in his State of the Union address, January 1823 and the Brezhnev Doctrine presented by Chairman Leonid Brezhnev in a speech in Warsaw, November 1968.

A comparison of the two doctrines is revealing.

The Monroe Doctrine—which has been reaffirmed several times in declarations by the Organization of American States [OAS]—declared that the U. S. shall oppose , "(1) any non-American action encroaching upon the political independence of American States under any guise; and (2) the acquisition in any manner of control of additional territory in the western hemisphere by any non-American power. . . . It does not imply, or countenance, a policy of aggression. It does not infringe upon the independence and sovereignty of the American States."

The purpose of the Monroe Doctrine, therefore, was not to impose a form of government on Latin American states, but to preserve the independence of those states and to provide for political pluralism in the region. It opposed re-colonization.

Some may argue that the Monroe Doctrine is ancient history and no longer applicable. The fact is that modern pronouncements by hemispheric organizations not only reinforce that Doctrine, but oppose the Brezhnev doctrine. . . .

The Brezhnev Doctrine reads: "When internal and external forces that are hostile to socialism (read 'communism') try to turn the development of some socialist country towards the restoration of a capitalistic regime, when socialism in that country and the socialist community as a whole are threatened, it becomes not only a problem of the country concerned but a common problem of all socialist countries. . . . Naturally, such an action as military assistance to a fraternal country designed to avert the threat to the social system is an extraordinary step, dictated by necessity." (The entire Brezhnev speech may be found in: L. I. Brezhnev: Following Lenin's Course [Moscow: Progress Publishers, 1972]).

In short, once a socialist state, always a socialist state. The massive military buildup now going on in Nicaragua signals a Soviet commitment to the enforcement of the Brezhnev Doctrine in the Caribbean Basin.

Why the Indecision?

It is appropriate to ask why Administration and Congressional policymakers are having difficulty arriving at U. S. policy for the Caribbean Basin. A Presidential Commission has been created to help in the task. Has the difficulty been that our policymakers do not understand the nature of the doctrinal conflict, or understanding it, are not prepared to enforce the Monroe Doctrine and oppose the Brezhnev Doctrine in this hemisphere? If not, has Soviet *disinformation* confused their perception?

Is there a lack of public support for enforcing the Monroe Doctrine and opposing the Brezhnev Doctrine because of ignorance or the failure of the government to be candid with the people? Or, is the problem simply that the country is still held in the grasp of a post-Vietnam trauma?

What must be clearly understood by all Americans is that the Brezhnev Doctrine means that no internal force, such as the "contra" revolutionary movement operating out of Honduras, or an external force, such as the U. S. or OAS military power, will be allowed by the Soviet Union to unseat the Sandinista movement and replace it with a democratic government. This means that we face a showdown between doctrines.

If the U. S. and the non-communist states of the Caribbean Basin tolerate the Sandinista government, as they have tolerated the Castro government, then they will be signifying their acceptance of the reach of the Brezhnev Doctrine into the Western Hemisphere. If those countries reject the Doctrine and seek to remove the Sandinista government by whatever means, they must be prepared to meet and repel a Soviet-supported military campaign to protect the Sandinista government.

In the light of the Monroe Doctrine and the confirming OAS policy statements, the U. S. has the authority for positive action. . . .

Propaganda and Disinformation

In large part, the government and the American people are having difficulty understanding the conflict in the Caribbean Basin because of skillful propaganda and disinformation produced by the Soviet Union to confuse the American people and to separate the U. S. from its allies in both the Western Hemisphere and in Europe.

In the Western Hemisphere that campaign has created dismay, distrust, and inactivity; and it has impeded forceful action on our part. No propaganda line has been more effective in this country than the comparison of Central America with Vietnam. The trauma that remains from our failed venture is being exploited by journalists, eager to get readers from headline to byline and into the lead paragraph. They hung innumerable stories about Central America on the "hook" of Vietnam—and in the process they have aided the Soviets in the extension of their empire into the Western Hemisphere. . . .

Cuba

Cuba is the immediate *"source"* of the current conflict in the

Caribbean Basin. It is the agent of Soviet expansionism. When Fidel Castro came to power in 1959, few Americans foresaw the significant factor Cuba would become in the world's strategic equation.

The U.S. made a colossal mistake by not insuring victory for the forces of Cuban and Caribbean volunteers at the Bay of Pigs [a military expedition the Eisenhower-Nixon adminis-tra-tion had prepared to invade Cuba and overthrow the Castro government. But John Kennedy became President before that project could be carried out. Kennedy attempted half-heartedly to go ahead with the project, but after a landing had been made, he withheld air support, and it all ended in failure]. Although Khrushchev's retreat in the Cuban missile crisis of October 1962 offset to some degree the ignominy created by that failure, a dispassionate analysis of the Ken-nedy-Khrushchev agreement which followed the crisis would reveal a second U.S. mistake, a foreign policy mistake. In that agreement the U.S. accepted the Castro regime. *Kennedy promised the Soviets not to invade Cuba and to restrain other Latin American countries from overthrowing Castro in exchange for the removal of ballastic missiles and IL-bombers.* [In retrospect we see that as one of the most colossal mistakes ever made by an American president]. In essence, Kennedy accepted in ad-vance the principle of the Brezhnev Doctrine in the Caribbean. [Later Khrushchev boasted: *It was a great victory for us, though, that we had been able to extract from Kennedy a promise that neither America nor any of her allies would invade Cuba.*]

Soviet Violations of the Kennedy-Khrushchev Agreement

After the enunciation of the Brezhnev Doctrine in Warsaw, the Soviets began to break the Kennedy-Khrushchev agreement by deploying new offensive weapon systems in Cuba. The first MiG aircraft came shortly after the Soviet invasion of Czechoslovakia.

The U.S. has objected to Soviet violations on several oc-casions, but in each instance the U.S. finally accepted the Soviet position. For example, the U.S. accepted Soviet assurances that its submarine base at Cienfuegos was not a naval base and therefore was not a violation of the agreement. The U. S. also accepted Soviet declarations that MiG fighters were for defensive purposes only and did not have a ground-attack mission.

Yet submarines armed with both ballistic missiles and cruise missiles operate out of Cienfuegos, and the MiG-23 Floggers have a far greater offensive capacity against U. S. targets than the IL-28 bombers in 1962.

★   ★   ★

Such, in part, is the warning presented in the *Washington Report* of the American Security Council. Surely this council has rendered a very valuable service in bringing before us the danger that we face. The question is, What are we going to do about it? Grenada was rescued from the Communists in 1983. But we did not follow through after that bold action. What most people do not know is that there are other hot spots in the Caribbean. Guyana, which is a small country on the northern coast of South America, has gradually turned toward the Communist side. Already it has Cuban-built airbases. Some of the Christians are being persecuted. And Suriname, another small South American country, which has a common border with Guyana, has moved in that direction despite several counter-coup attempts. Because our interest has been focused on the nearer countries, we have heard but little about those developments.

But at the present time, Nicaragua presents the most serious problem. We need to remind ourselves that in 1979, during the Carter administration, Russian- and Cuban-sponsored guerrillas, known as Sandinistas, overthrew the government and established a second Communist base, this time on the mainland of Central America. Since that time they have trained a large army, several times larger than the armies of all of the other Central American countries combined. They have built military bases and airfields and have received shipload after shipload of military supplies from Russia, including tanks, trucks, anti-aircraft guns, artillery, and aircraft. Their first objective soon became clear as they moved tons of military equipment into El Salvador to help the Marxist guerrillas who were trying to overthrow that government. That fighting is still going on. We have given limited aid to El Salvador. But it is clear that if we do not continue that aid or take some other action, the guerrillas are sure to win.

The larger question is whether or not the United States and the Organization of American States can find a way, diplomatic or military, to protect existing non-Communist governments from revolutionary takeovers—and eventually bring back into the organization those two nations that have turned Communist. The Soviets are working to turn all of the Central American nations into another Cuba. Certainly we cannot bail out those small nations one at a time as the emergency arises. Such a policy would have no end and would bankrupt our nation. Sooner or later we are going to have to go to the source of that trouble and have a showdown with Russia. Certainly we should support our President in his determined stand to strengthen our defenses. Otherwise it will mean the end of our way of life.